THOMAS C. GRELLA

Lessons in Leadership
Essential Skills for Lawyers

ABA LAW PRACTICE MANAGEMENT SECTION
MARKETING • MANAGEMENT • TECHNOLOGY • FINANCE

Commitment to Quality: The Law Practice Management Section is committed to quality in our publications. Our authors are experienced practitioners in their fields. Prior to publication, the contents of all our books are rigorously reviewed by experts to ensure the highest quality product and presentation. Because we are committed to serving our readers' needs, we welcome your feedback on how we can improve future editions of this book.

Cover design by RIPE Creative, Inc.

Nothing contained in this book is to be considered as the rendering of legal advice for specific cases, and readers are responsible for obtaining such advice from their own legal counsel. This book and any forms and agreements herein are intended for educational and informational purposes only.

The products and services mentioned in this publication are under trademark or service-mark protection. Product and service names and terms are used throughout only in an editorial fashion, to the benefit of the product manufacturer or service provider, with no intention of infringement. Use of a product or service name or term in this publication should not be regarded as affecting the validity of any trademark or service mark.

The Law Practice Management Section of the American Bar Association offers an educational program for lawyers in practice. Books and other materials are published in furtherance of that program. Authors and editors of publications may express their own legal interpretations and opinions, which are not necessarily those of either the American Bar Association or the Law Practice Management Section unless adopted pursuant to the bylaws of the Association. The opinions expressed do not reflect in any way a position of the Section or the American Bar Association, nor do the positions of the Section or the American Bar Association necessarily reflect the opinions of the author.

© 2013 American Bar Association. All rights reserved.

Printed in the United States of America.

17 16 15 14 13   5 4 3 2 1

Library of Congress Cataloging-in-Publication Data

Grella, Thomas C.
  Lessons in leadership : essential skills for lawyers / Thomas C. Grella.
  pages cm
  Includes index.
  ISBN 978-1-61438-816-6
  1. Practice of law--United States. 2. Leadership--United States. I. Title.
  KF300.G74 2013
  340.068'4--dc23
                                                                 2013021060

Discounts are available for books ordered in bulk. Special consideration is given to state bars, CLE programs, and other bar-related organizations. Inquire at Book Publishing, American Bar Association, 321 North Clark Street, Chicago, Illinois 60654-7598.

www.ShopABA.org

Contents

About the Author .... *vii*
Acknowledgments .... *ix*
Foreword .... *xiii*
Introduction .... *xvii*

Chapter 1 What Is Leadership? **1**

  Lesson 1 Position vs. Leadership 3
  Lesson 2 Servant Leadership 8
  Lesson 3 Empowering or Controlling:
             What Kind of a Leader are You? 14
  Lesson 4 Delegation in Practice—Leadership Teams in Law Firms .. 20

Chapter 2 Leadership and Management as Applied to the Law Firm **27**

  Lesson 5 Law Firm Management and Leadership of the Past 30
  Lesson 6 The Root Causes of Law Firm Failure—
             Leadership Failure.. 36
  Lesson 7 Emerging Trends Affecting Law Firm Leadership............ 40

Chapter 3 Development of Personal Leadership Skills 49

- Discipline 1 Passion and Focus 50
- **Lesson 8** Define Reality... 53
- **Lesson 9** Coaches and Mentors 59
- **Lesson 10** Education Plan 66
- Discipline 2 Balance 72
- **Lesson 11** Time Management... 74
- **Lesson 12** Leadership Communication 80
- **Lesson 13** Alone Time... 86
- **Lesson 14** Time Off... 91
- **Lesson 15** Strengths vs. Weaknesses............................ 97
- Discipline 3 Success.. 101
- **Lesson 16** Failure Is Not the Opposite of Success 103
- **Lesson 17** Learn from the Past—
  Honor and Respect Proven Leaders 108
- **Lesson 18** Be Driven by the Desire to See Others Succeed........... 112
- Discipline 4 Fulfillment 116
- **Lesson 19** Leadership Should Be Fun........................... 118
- **Lesson 20** Finding Your Authentic Voice 124
- **Lesson 21** Safety, Power, and Trust in Your Presence.................. 129

Chapter 4 Trust and Autonomy 135

- **Lesson 22** A Leader's Courage Is the Foundation of Trust........... 138
- **Lesson 23** The Varying Roles and Relationships of
  Members of a Law Firm 144
- **Lesson 24** Diversity and Gender 151
- **Lesson 25** Rules and Procedures: Carrots and Sticks.................. 156
- **Lesson 26** Dealing with Conflict................................... 161

Chapter 5 Leadership in Practice: Client Relations 165

- **Lesson 27** Influencing Clients—Leadership as the
  Key Role of a Lawyer 167
- **Lesson 28** Education of Firm Lawyers in the
  Skills of Leading Clients.. 173

Chapter 6   Day-to-Day Leadership   179
Lesson 29 Dealing With Personnel Issues 181
Lesson 30 Ethics and the Rules of Professional Conduct 188

Chapter 7   Strategy and Planning—Casting Vision   195
Lesson 31 The Role of the Firm Leader in Strategic Planning 198
Lesson 32 The Process of Strategic Planning—Is It for Everyone?.. 203

Chapter 8   Leading through a Crisis   211
Lesson 33 Strength and Courage in Times of Trouble 211

Chapter 9 Succession Planning: Leaving a Legacy for the Next Generation   219
Lesson 34 Planning to Plan 221
Lesson 35 Planning for Growth... 228
Lesson 36 Planning for Retirement—Succession of a Practice 238
Lesson 37 Planning for Management Succession 244

Conclusion   249

Index   251

About the Author

Thomas C. Grella is the Immediate Past Chair of the Management Committee of McGuire, Wood & Bissette, P.A. of Asheville, North Carolina, having served in that capacity for twelve years and having practiced law there for over twenty-five years. He continues to serve as ex-officio to his firm's Management Committee, and also serves as a member of its Strategic Planning Committee.

He has a JD from Wake Forest University Law School of Winston-Salem, NC and has been licensed as an attorney in North Carolina since 1985. He is a past Chair of the ABA Law Practice Management Section and has served in many positions within the Section, including being a member of its Council, Chair of its Core Groups, a member of its Publications and Magazine Boards, and Chair of its Diversity Committee. He is currently a Section Delegate, serving a three-year term in the ABA House of Delegates, and is Immediate Past Chair and a Member of the ABA House Technology and Communications Committee. He currently serves as columns editor of ABA LPM's Law Practice magazine. Tom was the 2012 recipient of the Sam Smith Award, presented annually by the ABA Law Practice Management Section to an individual who has demonstrated excellence in law practice management.

He is also a Fellow of the College of Law Practice Management, a Fellow of the National Institute for the Teaching of Ethics and Professionalism, and a Fellow of the American Bar Foundation. He is also a member of the advisory board of the Managing Partner Forum and a member of the Corporate Practice Group of his law firm. His practice focuses primarily on business entity formation, acquisitions and private placements of securities, home and property owner association representation, commercial transactions and leasing, and condominium law.

Grella co-authored *The Lawyer's Guide to Strategic Planning*, an ABA Law Practice Management Section publication.

Acknowledgments

Many of my friends have contributed, both directly and indirectly, to this book. Leadership principles have been around much longer than have I, and I have benefited from the talent and wisdom of many whom I know and some whom I have never even met.

As to those I do know, the list is long. First and foremost I thank my family. Writing a book is a time-consuming process. Much of the time I have spent in writing is time that I could have been spending with them. I am most appreciative of the loving support of my wife, Elaine, and daughter, Rebekah. I also thank my father and mother, Al and Delores Grella, as well as my mother- and father-in-law, Al and Fran Creasy, for all the love and support over so many years.

I want to give special thanks to those in my law firm, not just for giving me the opportunity to lead the firm over the last twelve years, but for the support they have given me over that time. I am especially appreciative of the great management committee at my firm, McGuire, Wood & Bissette, P.A. After years of working together, our collective failures and successes have helped teach us how to lead lawyers. Specifically, I would like to recognize a few people to whom I am very grateful but who are no longer with my firm: my former managing partners, the late Dick Wood, and my former firm administrators, George Leloudis and Mike Hudkins (with whom I coauthored the LPM publication *The Lawyer's Guide to Strategic Planning*). I also very much appreciate the support of our current managing partner, Doug Wilson.

I want to give a special thanks to my partner Lou Bissette. He has become a mentor in many ways, as well as a friend and confidant. Because we each have very different strengths and weaknesses, we complement each other well.

I am also deeply thankful for the special six-year relationship I had with Ed Flitton, prior to his untimely passing in 2010. His informal coaching and mentoring taught me so much about leadership of law firms that I am not certain that I would even have been able to write this book without it. We all miss him so much.

I also would like to thank Ken Crabb, the acting senior pastor of my church, Arden Presbyterian Church. Ken is an excellent leader and teaches a leadership principle almost every time he preaches. I appreciate the leadership he provides to my church and the lessons he has taught me over many years.

Of utmost importance, I want to thank the American Bar Association Law Practice Management Section. Without all of the relationships with practice management experts I have established through the section, I certainly would have never had the opportunities to lead that I have been blessed with over the years. I would like to thank the chair of the Publications Board, Tom Mighell, for his excellent leadership of the section and current board. Tom is one of the hardest workers that I know, and it was a pleasure to submit this publication to a board that he leads. I also want to thank Denise Constantine, our staff director of publishing, as well as her team. I also thank project manager Arthur Greene for his support, and publishing board member Jennifer Ator, who pushed me hard to write this book. Without her confidence and encouragement during the early stages of development, this book would have never been written. And a second thank-you to Tom Mighell and Jennifer Ator for their prepublication peer review.

The Law Practice Management Section is so very important to me. It has been instrumental in my development as a leader of lawyers and legal professionals. I would therefore be remiss if I did not recognize the section staff generally. They are a team of effective people, led by a very able director, Pam McDevitt. I thank them, and Pam specifically, for the hard work they provide to our members on a regular basis.

Finally, I want to make sure to recognize the many people who have been instrumental in helping with my leadership development; experts I have never met before. Each of the authors I have quoted or used as a suggested resource, have, through their expertise, mentored me in a unique way over many years. A few I have learned from at leadership conferences, and some I have learned from by reading their books and other writings. All have been quite helpful, and I them owe a huge debt of gratitude.

Foreword

On May 29, 1953, New Zealand's Edmund Hillary and his Nepali Sherpa, Tenzing Norgay, reached the summit of Mount Everest and made history as the first known climbers to ascend to the highest point on Earth. They faced mind-numbing cold, huge crevasses of ice and rock, and a limited window of suitable weather for their journey to the top. John Hunt led them there.

Hunt did not receive the media attention or glory that Hillary did, but his role in this historic climb cannot be understated. With the French and the Swiss set to attempt their own expeditions, the British faced intense pressure to reach Everest's peak first. Hunt was not the conventional choice to lead the British group, but organizers believed his military and climbing experience would help the group succeed.

For six weeks, Hunt expertly orchestrated the climb, selecting the right equipment, making the appropriate scientific calculations, and promoting efficient teamwork among his men. Hunt was within four hundred feet of the top, but he did not complete the ascent even though he was certainly experienced enough to do so. He chose a member of his team, Hillary, because Hunt believed he was better qualified for the task. Hunt put the objective and the mission first. That's what a leader does. It's service before self.

This concept is an integral part of Tom Grella's outstanding book *Lessons in Leadership: Essential Skills for Lawyers*. It is fitting that Tom would write about this subject for the American Bar Association. Tom is someone who takes a leadership role no matter the setting. A quick look at his life story tells you that Tom leads not just at his law firm but in his community, his church, his local and state bar associations, and the American Bar Association.

As a former chair of the ABA Law Practice Management Section and a member of our House of Delegates, Tom is widely admired and respected. Our members frequently seek his counsel on important issues, and he has led the section's executive committee through some challenging times.

In this book, Tom outlines principles he believes are critical for successful leaders of a law firm, whether it's a small office or one with thousands of employees. He explains his own successes (and failures!) as the managing partner of McGuire, Wood & Bissette in Asheville, North Carolina, and he discusses what works, what does not, and, most important, why. Through his stories, we understand the challenges of managing a firm, and we learn from his personal experiences. Tom shares his life lessons with us all—another example of service before self.

Tom's book is a compelling read for many reasons. There are thousands of books on the topic of leadership, but few focus on the special qualities of the legal field. To lead a law firm filled with partners, associates, and support staff is an often trying and very delicate balancing act. Leadership skills that may apply elsewhere may not be applicable to a law firm environment. Tom's book addresses this predicament by providing concrete examples, compelling anecdotes, and common-sense advice. The book identifies specific topics—then offers individual lessons and principles to live by. Tom also provides helpful links to additional resources and follow-up questions for reflection.

The next generation of law firm leaders needs mentors, and I am pleased to see Tom address this topic in Chapter 3. The best leaders mentor others and impart their wisdom and experiences. Consider Tom Watson Sr., who began his working life in Buffalo, New York, as a cash register salesman. He did not sell a single register in the first two weeks. At that point, his boss verbally ripped him apart. Watson was on the verge of quitting when his boss said, "Look. I realize you haven't caught on yet, and that's my responsibility. When people who work for me don't understand their job, I roll up my sleeves and I show them how." For the next week, the supervisor traveled with Watson, and together they sold three cash registers. Watson soon became the top regional salesman for that company. And he used the skills he learned as a salesman to form IBM, which became a dynamic, highly successful international corporation. Watson's son, Tom Watson Jr., who also headed IBM, recalled a favorite saying from his father: "A manager is an assistant to his men."

Leadership is not about simply being in a position where people say "She's in charge." Leaders take charge. They blaze a trail and help bring out the best in others. They bring professionalism, respect, integrity, discipline, and enthusiasm to every task.

Benjamin Franklin once said, "If you would not be forgotten . . . either write things worth reading, or do things worth the writing." Tom Grella has accomplished these goals in his book and in his career. The ABA draws extraordinary strength from members like Tom, who are willing not only to serve our fellow members but also to improve the profession. We are very grateful for this outstanding contribution to the field of law practice management.

Jack L. Rives
Executive Director
American Bar Association

Introduction[1]

Leadership is a reciprocal process between those who aspire to lead and those who choose to follow.

—James M. Kouzes and Barry Z. Posner[2]

My experience with leadership is best described with two clichés: baptism by fire, and three steps forward, two steps back. It was about twelve years ago when the two elder statesmen of my law firm came into my office to discuss my future with the firm. No, they were not coming in to fire me but to inform me that they wanted me to serve as chair of our management committee. Another firm partner had just stepped down after two years, and I was being tagged as the person to take over. That short meeting changed my life. It certainly affected everything that I would do or be involved in for the next twelve years.

The two partners indicated that my years in the Law Practice Management Section of the American Bar Association had served me well. I had become knowledgeable in the key areas of law practice management—finance, management, marketing, and technology—so I was the logical choice for the position. That was all well and good; however, there was just one problem. Though the title of the job was technically Chair of the Management

---

1. Throughout this book full citations are in the Suggested Reading section following the quotation.
2. *The Leadership Challenge*, page 23.

Committee and normally referred to as Managing Partner, practically it was a leadership position, and I knew very little about leadership.

What followed was twelve years of "managing" my law firm. I came to discover that not only are lawyers difficult to manage, they are even more difficult to lead. Through the many years since, I have become a student of leadership. I have experienced many management and leadership failures, as well as some important successes. I have also had the opportunity to help friends throughout the country navigate leadership roles in their own law firms.

The chapters in this book are organized into lessons, and one chapter is divided into four parts, each with lessons. Most chapters have introductions. Lessons have similar outlines; they begin with one or two quotes followed by an experience, example, or reference chosen to originate thought about the topic. Next are several leadership principles, followed by questions for you to consider about how the lesson applies to your personal and professional roles. Each lesson concludes with at least two suggested readings, books that I have read at least once or twice.

Although my perspective is that of a managing partner of a relatively small firm in a fairly small city in North Carolina, it is my strong belief that leadership principles are truly universal. Although the structure of a professional services organization, such as a law practice, is typical, leadership principles apply in a unique way. Every one of us—associate, partner, practice group leader, member of a firm management committee, executive director, or managing partner—is called to be a leader at some time. The leadership principles are basically the same whether your law firm has two members or two thousand. The principles in this book apply to each of us regardless of our title.

Leadership principles are easy to understand but very difficult to apply, especially in law firms. I say this to point out that you should "do what I say, as opposed to what I did." At times, I have certainly not shown exemplary leadership; however, my twelve years of managing a law firm and interacting with other law firm leaders have taught me what works, what does not, and why. As you read, you might think that the examples are all about my firm. They are not. Some are based on my firm (and I identify those); however, many are loosely based on my observations and experience giving advice to leaders of other firms. Unless I specifically indicate otherwise, the examples in this book are intended to be fictional and may be based on composites of firms or individuals.

It is my hope that this book can be an educational tool. I am a strong believer that each of us should have a time set aside each day (or at least often and regularly) for leadership education and training. In this book, I call that self-appointment Alone Time. This book is written so that you can use it during these times of study and reflection. Each lesson is intended to take about fifteen minutes to read and a few more minutes to consider the questions as applied to your circumstances. I highly recommend the suggested readings in the book, which, together with the wisdom of those who have taught me, have been a significant part of my education.

Suggested Reading

James M. Kouzes and Barry Z. Posner, *The Leadership Challenge* (San Francisco: John Wiley & Sons, 2002).

Bill George with Peter Sims, *True North: Discover your Authentic Leadership* (San Francisco: John Wiley & Sons, 2007).

Chapter 1
WHAT IS LEADERSHIP?

Leadership is influence—nothing more, nothing less.

—John C. Maxwell[3]

John Maxwell's quote is one of the simplest truths of leadership. Almost everyone can be a leader, and almost everyone *is* a leader to some extent, in some area of life; however, people are not "natural leaders" when they are born. Leadership is a skill that can be learned and developed. Leaders are found in every walk of life. Leadership does not come from a position or title. It is a result of influence over the conduct and action of others. Are people following your lead? If so, you are a leader. Management and leadership are not the same. Though it is helpful for a person in management to be a good leader, managers may manage competently without leading. Effective leaders are not necessarily good managers, but they usually know how to surround themselves with others who are.

There are many theories of leadership. The one that leads to the greatest success is "servant leadership." Although the ideas seem contradictory—being expected to be out front as well as serving those who follow—success as a leader always depends on how well a leader serves others.

---

3. *The 21 Irrefutable Laws of Leadership,* page 17.

Politics likely skews our views on the nature of true leadership and causes people to associate leadership with position, power, and authority. It is true that some people in positions of authority may wield power mercilessly, which may help them be effective, but power does not make them good leaders. Leadership is about influence, not force. Those who "lead" by force and intimidation, with a theoretical gun to the head of others, are not leading at all. A true leader uses a common mission, purpose, and vision—not threats or force—to move followers to act.

One of the best ways to exert leadership influence over others is to make them feel empowered. From executive or management committees to teams of members who work together to achieve some small part of the law firm's mission, delegating authority to others and empowering them to take meaningful action to further a common mission is crucial.

Lawyers need to understand that what we do in the legal profession is really, at the core, all about leadership. From influencing a client to decision making by a management team heading up the firm, in the words of John Maxwell: "Everything rises and falls on leadership."

Suggested Reading

John C. Maxwell, *The 21 Irrefutable Laws of Leadership* (Nashville: Thomas Nelson Publishers, 1998).

James L. Garlow, *The 21 Irrefutable Laws of Leadership Tested by Time* (Nashville: Thomas Nelson Publishers, 2002).

LESSON 1 POSITION VS. LEADERSHIP

> *Every profession and walk of life has its great figures, leaders and heroes . . . We exalt these individuals as role models and celebrate their achievements. They represent, we feel, the true model of leadership. But do they really? . . . [T]he most effective leaders are rarely public heroes. These men and women aren't high profile champions of causes, and don't want to be. They move patiently, carefully and incrementally. They do what is right—for their organization—for the people around them, and for themselves—inconspicuously and without casualties.*
>
> —Joseph L. Bardaracco Jr.[4]

A person in a position of management or authority is often tempted to exert the perceived power that logically seems to be attached to the role. This temptation can cause huge problems, especially for a new leader. I know this well because soon after I became chair of my law firm's management committee, I gave in to this impulse. I tried to force my colleagues to accept a new policy I thought was best for the organization. Before becoming chair of the firm's management committee, I had heard rumblings in my own corporate practice group about a perception that the firm did not have an appropriate policy to control the intake of new client matters. For some time I had had concerns about the firm's conflict-checking system. Others who were not in the litigation practice group had concerns that owners were not appropriately consulted about contingency cases and the commitment of our collective firm resources.

Soon after I became management committee chair, I spent a considerable amount of time drafting a client intake policy to deal with conflict-of-interest issues but it also went further, requiring a

---

4. *Leading Quietly: An Unorthodox Guide to Doing the Right Thing*, page 1.

special business conflict-check as well, and for certain matters, prior approval of the partners.

Some eleven years later, I still believe the content of that policy would be good for any firm to consider. In fact, a short time later I proposed a simplification to that policy, which is still in use today. I have also used the client intake policy as a model in publications. The real problem with the policy when I proposed it was not that it was substantively flawed (even if it was slightly modified later). The problem was that I had not consulted anyone before I put the policy out for consideration. I had not even consulted with the firm management committee. The response from the chair of our litigation practice group at the time was swift, direct, and completely justified. He rightly let me know that prior to my proposing policies that would have such a substantial effect on the way business was done in the litigation practice group, I should first seek counsel from not only the chair of the litigation practice group but also from the members of the management committee that the partners had elected to help me in proposing policies and procedures for the firm.

Today I'm grateful for this learning experience so early in my role. I learned a valuable lesson about using available resources (the management team) and the importance of collaboration. More important, I learned that I had not yet earned the trust of my partners, so I did not deserve to have them follow me, except out of duty. I learned that leadership does not come with position, just like wisdom does not come with age.

Leadership Thought and Application

When the honeymoon is over. There is a very short honeymoon period for a new leader. The prior leader may be honored, and you may be verbally lauded as the future. In reality, however, the people around you will be watching you like hawks. They will try to figure out what kind of leader you are going to be. If you happen to succeed a prior leader who was held in high esteem, your observers will undoubtedly make comparisons. Realize that as a new leader, you will make mistakes. It is inevitable. Don't seek them out, but when they happen, take advantage of them—they are opportunities for leadership and growth. Most of the early ones you make will be seen by others as instances where you are overstepping your bounds. They may have this view because you haven't yet won the trust necessary to make such bold steps.

Avoid the gallows. The alternative to learning from mistakes is not good. Firm owners will give their new leader enough rope to be hanged. Early on it is very important to understand that just as it is wrong for the owners who have elected you to make comparisons to prior seasoned leadership, it is also wrong for you to compare yourself to prior leaders. In fact, such comparisons are very dangerous to future success. A new leader should neither expect nor feel entitled to the same trust and respect enjoyed by the prior leader. These benefits are not entitlements that come with position. They are earned through successful leadership over many years of dedicated service.

Don't rely on position. Position is about authority, power, and right. Every person in a position of power and authority can certainly take these things by right. In contrast, leadership is about relationship, trust, and influence. Understanding this difference is key to successful leadership. Being a good leader is not an overnight achievement; it is hard work, but it is hard work in which all the progress you make can be lost in an instant. As a new leader, understand that the road to gaining the trust and respect of (and therefore being able to influence) followers in the firm takes time, and it comes in several different stages:

1. **Simple respect is afforded based on title.** Initially, all a new leader will be given is simple respect, mainly because the position deserves it, regardless of the occupant. Consider the statement about political leaders, where a member of one party has disdain for an elected leader: "Even though I

do not support the leader, I respect him." This is the only kind of respect that can be expected until the leader has earned some of the followers' trust.

2. **Being followed based on proven ability to achieve.** Once a new leader has achieved some success, others will follow because of the success. The extent to which they will follow depends on the level of the new leader's success.

3. **Trust based upon a sustained level of success.** A leader who has achieved long-term success can be counted on. Even a leader who makes mistakes is trusted to take advantage of a mistake and turn it into an opportunity. At this level, followers don't just follow; they trust the leader to act for the good of the organization and for good of each member.

Questions to Ponder

- In your own leadership, can you remember any mistakes that you have made by relying upon the power of position? If so, what lessons about leadership did you learn from the experiences?
- Think of a leader who you view as successful and one who you view as unsuccessful. How do you define success in viewing each of these examples? What qualities do you see in these individuals that have made them successful or unsuccessful in their positions of authority?
- Where are you on the spectrum of leadership? Are you followed because others simply give you the respect your position deserves at a minimum? Are you followed due to some level of achievement? Do you feel that you are truly trusted in your leadership? If the relationship is not yet one of trust, what steps can you take in your leadership to move closer to a trusting relationship with your followers?

Suggested Reading

Joseph L. Bardaracco Jr., *Leading Quietly: An Unorthodox Guide to Doing the Right Thing* (Boston: Harvard Business School Press, 2002).

Stephen F. Hayward, *Greatness: Reagan, Churchill & the Making of Extraordinary Leaders* (New York: Crown Forum, 2005).

LESSON 2 SERVANT LEADERSHIP

> [T]he great leader is seen as servant first, and that simple fact is the key to his greatness.
>
> —Robert K. Greenleaf[5]

After my first major leadership position was thrust upon me in 2001, I began to read and study many different principles and forms of leadership that existed at the time. In Appendix A to the first edition of his book *A Practical Guide to Leadership for Lawyers*, Herb Rubenstein documents ninety different "brands" of leadership in the marketplace, and he consolidates them into sixteen different categories.[6] Among all these types and categories of leadership was one that intrigued me: servant leadership. It was a very foreign concept to me. Almost all of the leadership examples I had encountered, even those who were seemingly selfless as it related to personal financial gain, appeared to need constant limelight, attention, and adulation. One who seemed different to me, however, was Richard A. Wood Jr., a former managing partner of my firm.

When I came to work in Asheville, North Carolina, in 1988, Dick had managed the firm for many years and would manage until he eventually stepped down at the end of 1999. When I joined the practice, it had only eight lawyers, although that number would eventually grow to more than twenty. I recall those first few months at the firm. My total receipt for billable work in my second month was only $800. That amount steadily increased, but certainly not by leaps and bounds at first, in my very transactional practice of law. Like clockwork, however, each month I would get my paycheck at the agreed-upon salary, as well a bonus at the end of the year,

---

5. *Servant Leadership: A Journey into the Nature of Legitimate Power & Greatness*, page 21.
6. Herb Rubenstein, *A Practical Guide to Leadership for Lawyers* (South Bend, IN: National Institute for Trial Advocacy, 2005).

regardless of the fact that my actual allocated collections certainly could not justify those amounts on a purely financial basis.

What I have come to realize is that each individual lawyer in a firm can bring much more value to the organization than what shows up on a financial statement. At the same time I also have come to realize that notwithstanding all of the other measures of value, to make payroll on a month-to-month basis, the bank account must be routinely repopulated with dollars. Times were quite tough for our firm back in the late '80s and early '90s, as they were for many law firms throughout the country. Only a few years later did I learn that in many of the months in which I was paid, the firm did not have the cash to pay all of its partners, associates, and staff, all of whom are legally employees of the corporate entity we call the firm. I also found out that without regard for his personal finances, Dick quietly loaned the firm, interest-free, the money needed to make payroll in those months, even though he was not obligated to do so. Dick believed that even though he did not have a legal obligation, firm leadership required his full support. He had a deep belief in our firm as the longest-operating law firm in western North Carolina, and he wanted to see it survive and succeed.

This is only one of the many examples of Dick's selfless service to the firm, acts that he chose not to broadcast. On many occasions Dick took time out of his very busy practice to tend to the needs of others. For example, he came to sit with my wife, Elaine, when I was in the hospital undergoing a very serious surgery. In the aftermath of that, Dick took it upon himself to inquire about my needs and assure me that the firm would support me while I was recuperating.

As a practice mentor, Dick understood that successfully completing a project was only half of the goal of an associate's work assignment. He always went the extra mile to assure that the project would contribute to the associate's professional development. In most cases the extra time and effort spent on the professional development was not credited as billable. I firmly believe that in the long run Dick knew that his many acts of service to the team would likely result in organizational success.

Dick retired from practice, and he recently passed away. I believe that he was aware how his acts of service would affect the firm beyond the time of his membership in it. Even though he knew he would not receive any short-term personal benefit, Dick was more concerned about the long-term success of others and the organization he loved.

Leadership Thought and Application

True servant leadership is about turning the typical organizational chart on its head. The structure of a typical law firm organizational chart is not usually the pyramid structure of most other business organizations. However, most law firms still have an informal, top-down hierarchy, one in which some members are considered subordinate, or subservient, to others. Notwithstanding this difficult organizational structure, applying the principle of servant leadership still works quite well.

Turning the organizational chart upside down is more easily said than done, however, especially in a law firm. It means that a leader must view his or her role as one of servitude to others and the organization. Consequently, a leader must realize that he or she will need to put the needs and concerns of others, and the firm, ahead of his or her personal goals, including goals related to time, financial gain, and other personal needs. Not everyone has the financial stability to make short-term loans to a firm to assure that payroll is met. Regardless, on a daily basis the true servant leader can find acts of genuine service to the firm and its members.

Some years ago I had the pleasure of attending a conference led by leadership speaker Ken Blanchard and his partner, Phil Hodges.[7]

---

7. "Lead Like Jesus," conducted by the Center for FaithWalk Leadership.

Ken Blanchard has written many books on leadership, success, ethics, and related topics to help business-people become more successful. In this conference, I learned some of the most basic principles about servant leadership. Since that time I have heard the same principles espoused by different speakers in different settings, so I am not sure of the true source of the principles. However, in their book *The Servant Leader*, Blanchard and Hodges point out that servant leadership is all about four applied principles, or characteristics, of a leader: Heart, Head, Hands, and Habits. As I have studied and pondered these four points, I have tried to apply them to my own leadership of clients, lawyers, staff, my law firm, and other organizations. Here is how I view these four principles as applied to leadership by a lawyer:

Heart. The principle here is all about motives. Am I in my position of influence for myself or for others? In the law firm setting, where lawyers are usually rated on many very objective financial criteria, the leader needs to ask whether decisions are being made for short-term personal profits and distributions or for the long-term viability of the firm. Regarding client work, is the lawyer leader making recommendations that achieve the best possible result for the client or ones that maximize productivity for the lawyer? Is the leader more interested in serving others or in making decisions that only serve the leader?

Head. This second concept is all about vision. The word *leader* itself assumes that someone is following. Without followers there's no leader. A leader must understand the organization's mission. A professional organization, such as a law firm, is not just about achieving profits. Every law firm is unique, and it needs a mission and a vision of how to get there. A lawyer leader must have in mind, for every client, member of the firm, and for the firm itself, an organizational purpose and the means to achieve that purpose. Firm leaders need to understand that their personal goals may be counter to the higher organizational purpose and that service to the firm can mean subordinating personal goals. Many lawyers believe that such business principles as mission, vision, values, and objectives don't apply to the profession of practicing law. In my experience, this is simply not the case. The lawyer leader needs to use his or her head and be able to articulate these strategic principles to all firm members and clients.

Hands. A leader's hands need to do what the heart demands and what the head knows to be the best for the firm and its clients and members. Knowing what needs to be done may be easy to determine, but mundane demands can keep a leader from taking necessary action. In many firms, the lawyer leader is expected to bill a multitude of hours in addition to fulfilling the role of leader. Because of established compensation systems, it is often a temptation to lead only when it is convenient. In these firms, what is called leadership is usually just management of day-to-day emergencies and problems.

Habit. Though a leader may do what the heart demands and what the head knows to be correct in a specific instance, the tendency is to address the immediate and not to look to the future. Perhaps it's human nature. Self-centered leadership seems to be a constant temptation unless the leader makes service to others a primary objective of regular action. To keep on track and focused on the mission and vision of the firm (which is usually achieved through a leader's selfless service to others), one must commit to good habits. In a law firm setting, these habits include activities such as (1) commitment to, and having, a regular time to study leadership, (2) practicing communication skills with all lawyers and staff in the firm, (3) committing to accountability through a coach or other trusted adviser, (4) seeking constructive feedback from all members of the firm, and (5) mentoring the next generation of firm leaders.

Questions to Ponder

- In your leadership, what is the primary motivation for your actions? Is it yourself, your family, the partners, all of the members of the firm? Is it to achieve a strategic purpose and goals, or is it some other objective?
- Does the principle of servant leadership make sense to you? If not, why not? What are some of the unique characteristics of a law firm that make servant leadership difficult? What can be done to change the environment in your own organization so that leadership through service to others can succeed?
- What day-to-day occurrences are most likely to keep you from moving forward in achieving the strategic mission for yourself, your clients, or your firm? What are some of the ways that you might address these occurrences so that they do not impede progress?
- What habits do you need to establish so that your service to the firm and its clients and members is the focus of day-to-day life?

Suggested Reading

Robert K. Greenleaf, *Servant Leadership: A Journey into the Nature of Legitimate Power & Greatness* (New York: Paulist Press, 1977).

Ken Jennings and John Stahl-Wert, *The Serving Leader: 5 Powerful Actions That Will Transform Your Team, Your Business and Your Community* (San Francisco: Berrett-Koehler, 2003).

Ken Blanchard and Phil Hodges, *The Servant Leader: Transforming Your Heart, Head, Hands & Habits* (Nashville: Thomas Nelson, 2003).

LESSON 3 EMPOWERING OR CONTROLLING: WHAT KIND OF A LEADER ARE YOU?

> *Giving orders and directions is not empowerment. Rather, an empowering leader trains, mentors, and apprentices someone to help him or her grow.*
>
> —Jeremie Kubicek[8]

I generally think of controlling leaders as people such as Hitler or Stalin. These are, in fact, extreme examples. Perhaps less extreme examples are U.S. presidents Andrew Jackson and Lyndon Johnson. The type of leadership I recommend in this book is not power of position. It is not about helping a leader understand how to be more controlling. Instead my focus is helping a lawyer leader be more effective for the firm through service to other members or the firm's clients, regardless of whether the leader is serving in a typical management role.

Controlling leadership is not seen only in the lives of politicians. When I graduated from law school, I went to work for a law firm where at first I was involved in only one aspect of discovery, particularly related to tobacco litigation. A team of about a hundred other lawyers and I coded documents for discovery. It was a tedious process. The members of the firm were not interested in innovation; they wanted assurance that their processes were maintained inviolate. They thought they needed young lawyers to follow the processes effectively. Nowadays this activity (which with the advent of technology no longer is done manually) would be sent overseas. I was not the only new lawyer who did not feel empowered in this work.

Controlling leadership can be a problem in any organization, but it may create greater risk in law firms. Consider this excerpt from

---

8. *Leadership Is Dead*, page 122.

the blog Above the Law, in which Susan Moon, an in-house lawyer, gives her observations about lawyers and control issues:[9]

> Most lawyers are supernaturally gifted at micromanaging. If micromanaging were a part of our job description, we'd be CEO in five and a half days. Lawyers also tend to be maddening perfectionists. Now put these two together into someone who manages other people, and bingo—it's like being attacked by a swarm of annoying, buzzing flies at the office. Only not so nice.
>
> We just have such a darned hard time letting go. Assuming that the person reporting to you is fairly competent, incessantly double-checking that person's work product often leads to one or both of the following undesirable situations: (1) the report's morale and confidence in his ability to do the job decreases; (2) the quality of his work product decreases because he knows that you will double-check everything anyway. This ends up making the both of you feel the need for you to continue to review and double-check everything. Our failure to trust the report perpetuates a situation that merits distrust.
>
> On the other hand, if you give a report full responsibility for a matter, a competent employee will begin to develop a sense of ownership for the work product. This will encourage increased attention to detail, since the report understands that no one else will be checking over the work.
>
> The problem is that it's really hard for people who are naturally micromanaging and perfectionistic to surrender full responsibility to someone else. Especially because we know that if there's ever an issue with the work product, we'll be the ones ultimately held accountable. Oh, did I mention that we're also just a teensy bit risk-averse?

---

9. Susan Moon, "Moonlighting: The Many Paradoxes of Managing Others," Above the Law (blog), May 4, 2012, http://abovethelaw.com/2012/05/moonlighting-the-many-paradoxes-of-managing-others/#more-155938.

Leadership Thought and Application

True leadership—positive influence over others—results only from mutual trust between leaders and followers. Mutual trust develops only if followers perceive that the leader has an honest desire to serve others. A leader can show this desire through actions and communications that show a significant part of the firm's mission is the growth of its members. Delegating significant responsibility to others—as well as an attitude that supports such delegation—leads to a type of empowerment that fosters personal growth and helps a leader mature and develop leadership skills.

It is natural for those entrusted with positions of leadership to want to oversee others and make important decisions. So how do they give up some of this responsibility and become leaders who empower others?

Trust. A leader must create an atmosphere in which mutual trust can grow, and that is easier said than done. Trust is cultivated over time and can be lost in an instant through indiscretion or mistakes. Consider the following trust builders:

1. **Examine your motives.** If a leader has personally selfish motives, delegating responsibility won't establish trust. To foster trust, be transparent and sincere in all you do.

2. **Make your word "stronger than oak."** In the movie *Jerry Maguire*, Tom Cruise portrays Jerry Maguire, a sports agent, and Beau Bridges plays Matt Cushman, the father of a football first-round draft pick. Cushman promises that although his son would not sign an agent contract, his word is "stronger than oak." That turns out to not be the case. Leaders must demonstrate that their words are truly "stronger than oak."

3. **Be consistent.** Effective leaders are consistent in both word and deed, and understand that the roles and needs of people in the firm differ. As a result, people are not treated equally,

but each person should be treated fairly and consistently. Consistency in your attitude and behavior is the base for establishing and maintaining trust.

Listen. Leaders are tempted to talk at or to others instead of talking *with* them. Telling people what to do and then letting them do it does not result in empowerment. Such delegation is perceived as a command, even if the person delegating does not closely monitor the activity. Instead, there should be a conversation. Identifying a problem and collaborating on a solution, with the leader giving enough authority, resources, and encouragement is empowering. A conversation certainly takes a greater commitment from a leader than simply giving a specific direction.

Consider practicing "listening verbalization" in your conversations. Instead of making demands or giving specific direction, have conversations. While the other person is talking, giving insight or suggestions, make a concerted effort to listen and recall what the person is saying instead of developing a response. When you practice listening verbalization, you recite back to speakers, immediately after they are done speaking, your recollection of what they just said to see if you heard them correctly. Only after you have confirmed that you heard correctly do you respond, continuing a collaborative discussion.

Be positive. Commit to having a positive attitude about all the members of the firm—their gifts, talents, and abilities. Armed with this positive attitude, give those you lead some rope in what you empower them to do and, to the extent possible, give them support so that they do not fall. If they do fall, however, help pick them up and, through your attitude, show them that the experience is an opportunity for education and growth that will lead to further opportunities to take a leadership role.

Maintain responsibility. Empowerment is not the type of delegation in which a leader loses responsibility for the actions of those who are empowered. One of the hardest parts of empowerment is the knowledge that although the leader gives up some decision making, the buck stops with him or her. The leader needs to be willing to take the heat for bad decisions and failures. Those being led are watching to see how a leader responds in tough times. A failure to accept ultimate responsibility for the team will make followers question the leader's true commitment to them, and it may destroy the ability to use empowerment to foster future organizational success—which is the goal.

Be authentic. Allow followers to be honest with you, and be honest with them. Such honesty is difficult in a law firm, largely because of the very flat organizational structure, with licensed lawyers on the top level and everyone else beneath. Those on that bottom level, even such professionals as a firm administrator who may be a certified public accountant, typically have cause (directly or through implication) to feel less valuable, perhaps like a serf in the law firm kingdom. Empowerment is about giving someone else the power not only to take action but also to speak up honestly without the fear of negative consequence. Authenticity needs to be understood as a two-way street. A leader must be willing to give up some power over subordinates and encourage other lawyers to understand the importance of doing so as well.

Questions to Ponder

- Do you have to personally approve every decision and control every activity of the firm? If so, or to the extent that you do, how does this tendency affect your ability to positively influence others?
- If you are a controlling leader, why do you feel the need to control others? What steps are you willing to commit to take to become a more empowering leader?

- Do you feel that you are generally open to new ideas brought forward by others?
- How do you feel when others in the firm have a good idea that you wish you had thought of? Do you first think of reasons not to move forward with the suggestion? If so, what steps can you commit to take in your own decision making and leadership so that the positive ideas of others have a fair chance to be implemented in the firm?

Suggested Reading

Jeremie Kubicek, *Leadership Is Dead* (New York: Howard Books, 2011).

Ken Blanchard and Phil Hodges, *The Servant Leader: Transforming Your Heart, Head, Hands & Habits* (Nashville: Thomas Nelson, 2003).

LESSON 4 DELEGATION IN PRACTICE—LEADERSHIP TEAMS IN LAW FIRMS

Clear instruction, confidence expressed as a high expectation, and an obvious trust in my ability to do the job. This was one of my earliest lessons in delegation.

—Max Depree[10]

While it was possible that his team of rivals would devour one another, Lincoln determined that 'he must risk the dangers of faction to overcome the dangers of rebellion.' . . . Later, Joseph Medill of the Chicago Tribune *asked Lincoln why he had chosen a cabinet comprised of enemies and opponents. He particularly questioned the president's selection of the three men who had been his chief rivals for the Republican nomination . . . Lincoln's answer was simple, straightforward, and shrewd. 'We needed the strongest men of the party in the Cabinet. We needed to hold our own people together. I had looked the party over and concluded that these were the very strongest men. Then I had no right to deprive the country of their services.'*

—Doris Kearns Goodwin[11]

Delegation and teamwork go hand in hand and are crucial in almost every endeavor. Regarding teamwork, the members of a team must complement each other and work together to be effective. Although it may not be a fair analogy, the Olympic 400-meter relay provides clear examples. In this race a smooth baton handoff is the key to success. In Beijing in 2008, both the U.S. men's and women's

---

10. *Leadership Jazz*, page 152.
11. *Team of Rivals: The Political Genius of Abraham Lincoln*, page 319.

Olympic teams dropped the baton and were disqualified. In London in 2012, the U.S. men's and women's teams both accomplished a very clean baton handoff. The men took silver, and the women gold. The difference between the 2008 and 2012 results was teamwork.

When I think of delegation by a leader, Dwight D. Eisenhower comes to mind. In early 1944, Eisenhower, the Supreme Allied Commander, planned extensively for the D-Day invasion as commander of Operation Overlord. He had spent much time solidifying relationships with other Allied leaders, including Churchill and Montgomery. He had also committed many hours to determining the strategic and tactical plans for the operation. Eisenhower was to remain in England, so every tactic had to be delegated. Unlike today, there was no instant communication, so Eisenhower could not adjust his orders after the invasion began. For that reason, he had to trust his team enough to delegate absolute authority to them. Because of the weather at sea and on the coast of France, difficult decisions had to be made immediately before the invasion. Ultimately, Eisenhower ordered the invasion. Knowing he had done his best to pick a team and delegate appropriately, Eisenhower gave the final order and had to wait to see if they would perform as expected.

In my experience in the practice of law and leading lawyers, I have seen successful and unsuccessful teamwork and effective and ineffective delegation. During the last twelve years, the management committee at my firm has included many different people. At times the committee has had a special synergy, and at other times that synergy is lacking. This lack of synergy usually results from a mismatch in the members' strengths and weaknesses. Delegation in my firm has been similarly uneven. Sometimes firm members are unwilling to truly delegate billable and administrative work. In fact, I have been guilty of this myself. This reluctance is usually a function of the perceived time commitment required to delegate, as well as a lack of trust in those to whom the task is delegated. On the other hand, I have seen people go overboard with delegation. Some partners will delegate so much of their billable work that one wonders if they themselves are doing any work at all. This is not necessarily a problem in and of itself, as in every firm there needs to be an effort to drive work down to lower levels where it can be performed at the lowest cost and expense (and therefore the highest margin). But unless the partner provides proper supervision and oversight and explains to the client why the matter has been delegated, trouble is usually the result.

Leadership Thought and Application

Using teams properly can be a significant factor in a firm's success. Good teamwork allows the leadership group to function well, and it allows firm members to perform client work effectively.

Teamwork and delegation of firm members. All members of the firm—lawyers and staff—should be encouraged to find ways to work in teams. In firms organized into practice groups, teamwork is probably the norm. However, a practice-group organization can promote cliques and factions, which work against firm-wide collaboration. To break down some of these barriers, firms may use client service teams. These teams include two or more professionals, each of whom may be a representative of a different practice group.

Regardless of the firm's organization, a firm leader's job is to encourage teamwork and delegation and create opportunities for members to work in teams. The following should be considered in establishing team opportunities:

1. **Encourage firm members to work in teams and provide opportunities.** A leader should communicate the importance of lawyers and staff working together on client work and other tasks that forward the firm's mission and vision, such as work on committees, planning groups, or specific task forces. At meetings of attorneys, staff, and partners,

attendees should be encouraged to volunteer for these opportunities.

2. **Match people on teams based on common interests.** Serving on a technology committee or a holiday planning committee is not a good fit for every firm member. The leader should appoint people based on experience and interest.

3. **Match people based on strengths and weaknesses.** If the team members have the same strengths and weaknesses, reaching conclusions that are in the best interest of the law firm will be difficult for them. The team dynamics will also suffer. A leader who organizes teams should strive for diverse strengths and weaknesses so that team members will tend to complement each other.

4. **Require accountability.** Team members should establish accountability systems for reporting to each other and procedures for periodic reporting to firm management. The team should report regularly and work to meet established deadlines.

5. **Give discretionary authority to take action.** Establishing teams for substantive and administrative work allows many people in the organization to shine, as long as those performing tasks are given some discretion to make decisions and to implement those decisions with authority.

In conclusion, law firm leaders should consider using teams for the following reasons:

- to teach firm members team building and the principles behind team success
- to show a leader's trust of others in the firm
- to build relationships between diverse members of the firm

Management Team Dynamics. As a leader, regardless of your specific position, using teams to accomplish the firm's mission is of utmost importance. Consider the following principles to build a strong effective team:

1. **Surround yourself with people who are strong in the areas where you are weak.** The members of a team must work well together, and they need strengths in different areas. Know your own strengths and weaknesses and appoint members who can bring missing strengths to the team.
2. **Delegate to fellow leaders.** Generally leaders want to monitor and even micromanage, especially when they might be held accountable for others' mistakes or failures. Even so, a leader must trust fellow leaders and delegate adequate authority to them so they feel empowered to act.
3. **Encourage full, free, and fair discussion within the team.** All team members must be confident that they can express opinions without consequences. The team leader's job is to instill this level of comfort in each member of the group.
4. **Support team decisions.** For a decision to be effective, each member of the team must support it, even if the issue was hotly debated and some members were strongly opposed to the decision during the discussion. A split runs a huge risk for others to divide the firm and defeat an initiative. This can be avoided if the management team sticks together and supports their decisions as a team.

Loyalty between and among members of a team is crucial, and a leader can build it by displaying the following qualities:

1. **Courage.** Leaders must sometimes take action when negative consequences—even those with a potentially greater impact on the leader than on the firm—are possible. Such courageous action builds trust in other team members.

When others in the firm become aware of courageous action, it builds trust in them as well.

2. **Confidence.** A leader's courageous action builds his or her confidence and fosters the confidence of others in the leader. This confidence helps create a sense of security throughout the firm.

3. **Trustworthiness.** Even though some management actions may seem casual, the leader's relationship to the firm is not. The members of the firm must see the leader as absolutely trustworthy and loyal, not as merely a leader for a set number of years. The relationship is that of a "counselor." It is a covenant, or promise, that the leader makes to others in the organization.

Questions to Ponder

- How well does the management of your firm work as a team? Are the decisions that your team makes supported by all of the members of the team, or does a split decision end in gossip and division?
- How well do you delegate to others? Does your delegation include empowerment or micromanagement?
- Is your committee a loyal team? Do you instill loyalty in your team?
- List the five things that you can do to better your leadership in the area of teamwork and delegation.

Suggested Reading

Max Depree, *Leadership Jazz* (New York: Bantam Doubleday Dell Publishing Group, 1992).

Doris Kearns Goodwin, *Team of Rivals: The Political Genius of Abraham Lincoln* (New York: Simon & Schuster, 2005).

Patrick Lencioni, *The Four Obsessions of an Extraordinary Executive* (San Francisco: Jossey-Bass, 2000).

John C. Maxwell, *The 17 Essential Qualities of a Team Player: Becoming the Kind of Person Every Team Wants* (Nashville: Thomas Nelson, 2003).

Chapter 2
LEADERSHIP AND MANAGEMENT AS APPLIED TO THE LAW FIRM

> [L]eadership has everything to do with character. Character is about doing the right thing. Leadership is about doing the right thing. It has even been suggested that managers do things right while leaders do the right thing.
>
> —James C. Hunter[12]

Some historians charge that the Great Depression was the fault of Herbert Hoover, then president, although he had been in office for just a year when the stock market crashed. However, it is unclear whether he should be blamed for what occurred in 1929 or whether he could have done much to turn the country around in the three remaining years of his term. I am a collector of books about U.S. presidents, and I believe much can be learned from presidential leadership, or lack thereof. *The Herbert Hoover Story*, by Eugene Lyons,[13] supports what I believe is the true reason that Herbert Hoover has been portrayed so negatively for more than eighty years. Considering Hoover's actions before and after he was in office—including actions not related to the Great Depression—Lyons's

---

12. *The World's Most Powerful Leadership Principle: How to Become a Servant Leader,* page 31.
13. Eugene Lyons, The Herbert Hoover Story (New York: Human Events, 1959), pages 22 and 27.

book supports that Hoover was one of our greatest public servant presidents:

> The implication is not that our thirty-first President is deficient in sound political judgment or in the grasp of political trends and strategies. He is a shrewd enough judge of men and over-all situations; a thousand times he has demonstrated in vital matters that he is an executive administrator and negotiator with few equals in his time... Where he falls short is in dexterity—in maneuvering people and making "deals" on the political plane; in selling himself and his policies to the crowd; in playing on mass emotion.... According to another historian, Allan Nevins, Hoover "can run a department or set of departments with great skill; he can organize forces to meet an emergency; but he cannot direct a party, lead a parliamentary group or guide public opinion."

Lyons points out that Hoover was not a good politician. Although Hoover was a good manager (outside of the presidency), a primary role of the position of president is leadership, and Hoover simply was not a good leader.

A continuing debate over many years has been whether the practice of law is a profession or a business. Some of us have answered that question with one word: both. An equally popular debate is whether leadership is different from management. In a profession like ours, which cries out for leadership in so many ways, it is interesting that leadership roles are often confused by identification with the word *management* (for example, managing partner and management committee).

Leadership and management are not one and the same. Management is about handling the day-to-day details—ensuring that things get done correctly and addressing problems that arise. Leadership entails much more: it is about taking the organization from one place (the present) to another (the future) and influencing the members of the organization to come along.

I believe that, as John Maxwell often says at his seminars and conferences, there are universal laws of leadership. At the same time, because of the unique control structure of most law firms (and similar professional organizations), these principles apply in a different way than they do in other business organizations. Lessons in this chapter will consider

1. changes in law firm management during the past thirty years and how these changes have affected law firm leadership,
2. the effect of leadership on a law firm's ability to succeed, and
3. emerging trends in law firm management and how they may affect a leader's ability to influence members of the law firm.

Suggested Reading

James C. Hunter, *The World's Most Powerful Leadership Principle: How to Become a Servant Leader* (New York: Crown Business, 2004).

Dale Carnegie, *How to Win Friends and Influence People* (New York: Simon & Shuster, 1936).

LESSON 5 LAW FIRM MANAGEMENT AND LEADERSHIP OF THE PAST

> *If it is a financial performance issue or a problem partner who is no longer doing quality work, you are the leader and must take charge. That does not mean that you necessarily drop all that you are doing at the moment (though it may). It means you have to give the problem the priority it deserves, address it in a timely fashion and follow-up on the solution.*
>
> —Robert Michael Greene[14]

In February 2012, I had the privilege of moderating a panel of managing partners of the five largest law firms in Delaware. The panel was assembled by the editors of *Delaware Lawyer*, and the topic of the roundtable was transformations in law firm management in Delaware over thirty years.[15] Those participating in the roundtable had generally been involved in some aspect of their law firm's management, and they all currently had the top position at their firm.

One of the most significant and broadly applicable points was made by William J. Wade, president of Richards, Layton & Finger, P.A. When asked about whether values of lawyers have changed over the years, he responded:

> It's more the expectations [that have changed]. When we all started, the expectation [was] the firm hired you, you would be an associate for a number of years and then you would be a partner and that would be great. I think that now people come in with different goals. Whether it's loyalty, or whether it's expectation, I think any given number of our beginning lawyers don't expect to be there long enough to become a partner. They want to gain the basic background and then move on to

---

14. *Managing Partner 101: A Primer on Firm Leadership*, pages 43–44.
15. For the full printed text of the discussion, see "An Anniversary Roundtable: Transformations in Law Firm Management," *Delaware Lawyer* 30, no. 1 (Spring/Summer 2012), pages 8–21.

something else, whether it's in house somewhere or a different kind of practice. We have people who take themselves out of the partnership track and say, "I love the place, I love the job, I love what I'm doing, but I don't want to be tied to the BlackBerry at all times, so I want to have lowered expectations and go along that way." So there are changes in people's expectations and they probably are driven by lifestyle balance, and people are willing to make that choice, whereas I don't think we were willing to make that choice as much in the past.

Several comments at the roundtable echoed this concept. Many of the management tools have changed, but at its core, management has not really changed in thirty years. The demands of leadership, however, have changed as the priorities of lawyers entering the practice have changed. Law firms that go through the process of strategic planning find that agreed-upon values have changed and that individual lawyers have changed how they prioritize those values. The job of the law firm leader still includes day-to-day management, but to a greater extent it involves leading a less homogeneous group: individuals' values and priorities may differ widely.

Leadership Thought and Application

Over the past thirty years, important aspects of the business organization of law firms have evolved. As a result, law firm leaders must consider the impact of this evolution on their ability to lead. At the same time, it is clear that people have not changed. Management principles are exactly the same; some are just applied differently. Consider a few of the changes:

Management structure. Firm leadership used to be very heavily concentrated at the top. More recently many firms have evolved to a more collaborative structure with an elected management committee. In some cases, a group of lawyers may leave a larger firm that is heavily top controlled to create a law firm with more collaborative governance. For the leader, it is simply a matter of changing priorities and focus.

For instance, though the law firm leader of thirty years ago was more likely a dictator (hopefully a benevolent one), each lawyer may have had almost complete autonomy over his or her practice. Today, though partners in law firms want a voice in firm management, law firm leaders realize that absolute individual autonomy should not be encouraged. Today's leadership challenge is to find ways to lead firm members into a collaborative team environment. This environment must enable the firm to achieve its strategic goals while allowing for a proper level of individual autonomy. It is important that firm members not feel overly restricted or burdened with unnecessary rules and procedures.

Recruitment of attorneys. Thirty years ago the priorities and expectations of lawyers entering the marketplace were homogenous. Lawyers expected to be hired for a career, and they expected extreme and mutual commitment and loyalty in the lawyer-firm relationship. This is no longer the case. On the law firm side, there are new means of expanding the firm, including merger and lateral hires (fueled by less of a long-term commitment to previous employers). Expansion also comes from hiring nonlawyer professional staff to perform unbundled functions of legal services. On the new lawyer side, there is a greater desire for positions that fit shorter-term personal goals instead of long-term commitment. The consequence is that leaders must be more in tune with new hires' values and priorities. If a leader is looking for long-term commitment and loyalty, traditional job qualifications may have to take a back seat. On the other hand, the law firm may need to change its view on traditional partnership criteria when looking for candidates, being up-front that either the firm is not as committed to the traditional partnership model or that it has been scrapped for something different.

Staff. In the not too distant past, law firms basically had three positions: lawyer, secretary, and one bookkeeper. Because every lawyer had a secretary, allocating expenses was fairly straightforward. Then law firms began hiring paralegals to perform some of the client service tasks that were beyond the secretary's ability, expertise, or available time. Over the years, the number of indirect support staff has expanded. Today's firm may have a firm administrator, financial officer, human resources administrator, technology administrator, librarian, facilities manager, records manager, intake manager, marketing administrator or staff, billing specialist, hospitality coordinator, or maintenance engineer. As these general support staff have been hired over the years, and as technological advances have accelerated, there has been a concerted effort by most firm leaders to reduce the ratio of secretaries or legal assistants to lawyer. For example, a law firm with a one-to-one ratio in the 1980s may now have a lawyer-to-legal assistant ratio of three or four to one. These changes have blurred the authority hierarchy within firms. In the past, leaders had a tendency to focus on the lawyer members and their needs. Now leaders must understand the differing needs and values of all members of the firm and lead everyone. Today law firms are much more diverse business organizations, and leadership is therefore more complex.

Value. In years past, determining the value of a member of a law firm and the value provided to a client was fairly simple. The value of an individual lawyer was based on billable hours, actual collections, or other fairly objective criteria. Nonbillable functions were uncompensated but verbally encouraged unless billing requirements were not met, in which case such activities were discouraged. The rationale was that nonbillable activities are important and are eventually reflected in increased hours or increased collections. As a result, the efforts encouraged were narrowly focused on individual short-term performance, not the organization's long-term success. Absent a client's active complaint, the value to the client was usually based on the amount of effort—billable hours—that the lawyer spent on the matter. Though many law firms of today still live in the past, some others have begun to understand that effort (or time) and value are not one and the same. These progressive organizations understand that law firms must no longer operate as individual businesses with a similar address, but as a single business made up of many different team members, many licensed, but some not. Value is seen in a more comprehensive way, not merely tied to objective numbers, but to subjective determinations of the importance of contribution to the firm's short-term success as well as its long-term viability.

Communication and information flow. Thirty years ago most of a firm's communication was through one of two means: paper copies (letters written to clients and sent by U.S. mail and memos written and distributed to firm members) and verbal exchanges (by phone or in face-to-face meetings). Today, communication within most firms is either oral (to those within hearing distance) or electronic. Some external communication may be through U.S. mail, face-to-face meetings, and phone calls, but most communication is electronic. Until recently, electronic communication generally meant e-mail, but lately it has grown to include intranet, extranet, and social media. Because of the ease of communicating—often without much thought about the content or consequences of the communication—leadership challenges have mounted. Because much of leadership success depends on what and how information is communicated, leaders must be skilled in these new forms of communication.

Questions to Ponder

- How has your firm's leadership structure changed over the years? Has the form of governance evolved? If so, is the structure of management and governance optimal at present?
- In what ways is your leadership, and that of other firm members in authority, out of date? What areas of improvement have top priority?
- Have the personal values or priorities of those coming to work for your firm changed over the last thirty years (or fewer if your firm is younger than thirty years)? How? In

what ways has the firm adapted to these changing demands? If the firm has not changed, how will it deal with the needs of new members?

Suggested Reading

Robert Michael Greene, *Managing Partner 101: A Primer on Firm Leadership* (Chicago: American Bar Association, 1990).

Peter F. Drucker, *The Effective Executive: The Definitive Guide to Getting the Right Things Done* (New York: Harper & Row, 1967).

LESSON 6 THE ROOT CAUSES OF LAW FIRM FAILURE—LEADERSHIP FAILURE

> *The good-to-great leaders never wanted to become larger-than-life heroes. They never aspire to be put on a pedestal or become unreachable icons. They were seemingly ordinary people quietly producing extraordinary results. . . . Level 5 leadership is not just about humility and honesty. It is equally about ferocious resolve, an almost stoic determination to do whatever needs to be done to make the company great.*
>
> —Jim Collins[16]

In January 2003, the national law firm of Brobeck, Phelger & Harrison shut down. In the years immediately before its demise, it had been seen as one of the nation's most successful law firms, one that had been ranked among the best places to work in the country. It had been run by a seemingly charismatic leader just before it went under. Several other large firms have failed since that time, including Howrey & Simon in March 2011 and, most notably, the firm of Dewey & LeBouf in May 2012. The Brobeck firm had been ranked as the twenty-second largest in the world by *American Lawyer Magazine* and had increased in size mainly by enticing lateral hires from other firms, with the promises of large salaries and bonuses. It is said that the firm collapsed due to extensive mismanagement, which extended to all areas of a flawed business model.

So the question is, with all of the talent in these huge and seemingly successful law firms, why did they fail? Could it all be blamed on the dot.com bust (Brobeck in the early 2000s) or a difficult economy (Howrey, Dewey, and others more recently)? In each firm, extrinsic factors certainly contributed to its downfall, and perhaps to the speed at which it succumbed to its inevitable failure.

---

16. *Good to Great*, pages 28 and 30.

Most articles describe the Brobeck leader as charismatic and say large sums of money were spent on extravagant items and wasted on national television brand marketing. Some consultants may point to culture problems and a failed compensation system that did not adequately protect against partner defections.

Articles about Howrey may note that the firm expanded too much and too fast, opening offices that would never become profitable at a time when clients had begun to demand new billing systems and lower fees. As the firm rapidly grew larger, conflicts of interest limited matters that it could take on. Without the systemic loyalty required to sustain in the long term, the organization became a partnership in name only.

Articles about Dewey point to inconsistent partner-compensation systems (some "open" and some "closed"), a refusal to change with a changing economic environment, failed marketing plans, and an inability to understand the changing needs of the firm's employees.

Some reasons behind the failure of these and other firms are common and some unique, but generally the cause is failed leadership, which is a common cause of failure in other types of business organizations.

Leadership Thought and Application

Leadership is not a complicated or complex subject. The principles are quite easy to understand; it is effective application that proves difficult. John Maxwell is well-known for his twenty-one irrefutable laws of leadership, and his book with the same name explains each one. He believes that the leader who breaks any one of them (as with any law) will suffer some negative consequence. With each failed law firm of the past, one can point to leadership principles that have been violated.

One very common characteristic of failed organizations is that leaders do not tell the full truth to followers. Though they may give firm members information, it is usually incomplete because it does not provide a true picture of where the firm is, where is it's headed, and the obstacles and hazards it is likely to encounter along the way. Other common characteristics of organizations headed toward failure (law firms included):

1. **Leaders fail to recognize the needs of followers.** The leaders of the organization do not make it a priority to nurture followers—professionally or personally. Followers, feeling the lack of nurture, assume that the leaders are more interested in personal gain than in serving others.

2. **Leaders fail to encourage others in their work for the law firm.** A leader who lacks investment in others' important work precipitates feelings of discouragement and despair in those he or she leads.

3. **Leaders fail to give followers the necessary support.** As followers perform work for the firm, issues arise, and leaders do not provide support or even show a desire to provide it. In some cases, providing support would mean less of the leader's time, money, and effort for the firm's established priorities. In other cases, particularly in difficult times, a leader may support only the most successful members (lawyers with the strongest practices) in the belief that the strongest members will be able to help the leader get what he or she wants.

4. **Leaders fail to address practice-related or interpersonal issues that arise.** Some leaders may simply "look the other way" when systemic problems become evident. In some cases members may need strong and stern discipline. Other situations are caused by external factors over which members have no control. Ignoring either type of problem may stem from fear or inadequate concern. However, these types of issues rarely vanish on their own.

5. **Leaders do not address stray followers.** A true law firm is a team of professionals working toward a common mission, vision, and goals. Occasionally a member of the firm will stray from these common understandings. In many law firms, especially ones that have grown through the merger of a few very small firms, leaders must deal with the problem of members' personal autonomy. Although members may verbalize a common commitment to their mission, their actions show otherwise. The leader must be involved in directly addressing these personal autonomy problems when they arise.

Questions to Ponder

- Is your law firm a great law firm? If so, what makes it great? If not, why not?
- To what extent are you committed in your leadership to telling the members of the firm the truth about the condition of the firm? To what extent is the membership of your firm's professional staff, both lawyers and support personnel, engaged in discussion of the strengths, weaknesses, opportunities, and threats facing the firm?
- Do you see any of the characteristics of a failed law firm as problem areas for your own firm? If so, which ones, and what can you do proactively to address these concerns?

Suggested Reading

Jim Collins, *Good to Great* (New York: Harper-Collins, 2001).

John A. Barnes, *John F. Kennedy on Leadership: The Lessons and Legacy of a President* (New York: AMACOM, 2007).

LESSON 7 EMERGING TRENDS AFFECTING LAW FIRM LEADERSHIP

> *The leader of the Future is the Leader Integrator—an individual who breeds multiple perspectives, consciously connecting these perspectives and applying a variety of skills to establish new directions, options, and solutions for the organization.*
>
> —Usman A. Ghani[17]

Predicting the future is a hard and dangerous business. Within my own law firm, the structure of management and formal leadership has changed considerably since January 4, 1988, my first day as an associate. Our small eight-person firm has gone from a benevolent dictatorship (where administrative functions were done by a bookkeeper who had started with the firm a few years before as a paralegal) to a system of management and leadership where a team of four members of an executive committee leads a firm of twenty-five lawyers, and a chief operating officer with a certified public accounting status leads a small team of administrative employees in the important functions of technology, finance, marketing, and management. As of the writing of this book, the firm is planning for changes that will eventually come our way; changes that will require a new vision and a new approach to decision making and leadership. The moves we have made so far, however, are fairly typical for law firms with similar positions of slow steady growth over a period of many years.

The changes down the road for most law firms, including my own, may not be all that typical. As larger law firms continue to fail and significant flaws in systems of lateral hiring become apparent, we are already seeing major shifts in law firm structure and

---

17. Frances Hesselbein and Marshall Goldsmith, eds., *The Leader of the Future 2*, page 243.

management. The law firm of Pepper Hamilton recently announced their decision to hire a CEO who is not a lawyer. It has become commonplace for nonlawyer firm administrators to take on the role of COO in a firm; however, Pepper Hamilton is one of the few firms where significant executive control is in the hands of a non-lawyer. The firm claims it still has a managing partner, but both operational and executive day-to-day decisions are delegated to a different organizational level. Is this the wave of the future?

Patrick McKenna, a well-known law firm consultant, sees a trend toward two lawyers sharing the position of managing partner so they can continue to have a substantial vibrant legal practice instead of devoting full time to management.[18] If this is a trend, it will certainly create leadership challenges. Without the best possible persons selected for such a comanagement marriage, members of the firm may become confused about lines of authority, and the two leaders may have difficulty managing each other. The two also may collectively spend more time managing the firm as a pair than either one would have spent as a sole managing partner.

Another current trend seems to be the failure of large firms. At the time of the writing of this book, a recent example was the Dewey & LeBeouf law firm, which filed for bankruptcy protection in mid-2012. (Failed leadership as a root cause for firm failure is discussed in greater detail in Chapter 7.) This trend of law firm failures is often partially blamed on the firm's lateral hiring practices and the corresponding promises of huge salaries and bonuses that are not justified under any sensible business model (which are themselves a result of failed leadership).

Lateral hiring, however, is not the only problem. Failing firms generally have not modernized; they have continued to operate as

---

18. Patrick McKenna, "The Trend Toward Having Co-Managing Partners," JDSupra® Law News, June 19, 2011, (http://www.jdsupra.com/legalnews/the-trend-toward-having-co-managing-part-94009/).

inefficiently as ever. Non-lawyer entrepreneurs have entered the legal market, and clients with a philosophy of "better, faster, cheaper" are satisfied to take their business elsewhere. Further, these alternate providers are no longer operating with inadequate expertise, as they in fact have been hiring some of the best and brightest. Talented young lawyers whose goals are different from lawyers who entered the marketplace in the 1970s and 1980s are more willing to make the leap to the lifestyle afforded by these new forms of legal service providers. While these new competitive forces were entering the marketplace, many larger law firms, maintaining what was either an elitist or ostrich mentality, seemed to ignore the possibility that the changes would ever have any negative repercussions on the way they do business. For many, that was a miscalculation.

These three nontraditional firms may provide a glimpse of the legal playing field of the future:

Novus Law (www.novuslaw.com) is an organization that specializes in electronic document management. Although this group seems to concentrate on the electronic discovery function, its website touts a special document management process for large companies in all functions that require documents, not just litigation. The founders of this law-related organization discovered that the services their cutting-edge technology allows them to provide are the same types of work formerly delegated to high-priced, big-firm associates. The leaders of Novus believe that the services their organization provides are better than those previously provided by large firms.

Axiom (www.axiomlaw.com) employs one thousand or more very talented lawyers, and many, if not most, of this multitude previously worked for large law firms. Axiom is a new type of law firm organization: it has quality talent, but no partners. Axiom founders recognize that legal matters are not all the same, but they claim that all legal work fits into one of three categories: exceptional events, matters requiring experience, or matters requiring efficient service.

Traditional firms consider that these categories each account for about the same volume of work, but they do not. Axiom believes that traditional law firms should use an organization like theirs (which uses advanced technologies and offers low-cost solutions) to perform lower-level efficiency work. Axiom's website has an extensive list of specific case studies of the ways it provides services, employing such means as unbundling litigation to provide discovery at lower costs. The organization also provides contract management services, due diligence in transactional work, and human resources consulting for such functions as benefits planning and compliance.

Morningstar Law Group (www.morningstarlawgroup.com) is certainly not a traditional firm. It is made up of ten lawyers, each of whom had a long tenure at one of a handful of the largest law firms in North Carolina. Some of Morningstar's stated values are fairly traditional; however, the firm describes itself as a true partnership, according to a statement on the firm's website:

> We are dedicated to creating a healthy, cohesive work environment among our attorneys. That means recognizing and rewarding a variety of contributions to the firm, treating attorneys in an equitable and respectful manner, and providing meaningful involvement in decision-making. We understand that attorneys and staff have a variety of lifestyle and family needs. We believe that focusing on creating a true partnership among our attorneys leads to higher productivity and better client service.

When Ken Carroll, one of the founders of the firm, was asked about this idea of true partnership in an interview, he stated:[19]

> The downside to centralized management is that it tends to create a sense of apathy and disenfranchisement among the working owners, i.e., equity partners, which I find troubling. You end up feeling like an employee rather than a business owner, and in fact you really are nothing

---

19. Mary E. Vandenack, "Dawn of a New Business Model," *Law Practice Magazine* 39, no. 1 (January/February 2013), pages 33–34.

more than an employee because you rarely ever are consulted about significant decisions in a meaningful way. We have 10 partners so far, and we sit around the table and discuss pretty much everything. . . . In our early discussion about the possibility of forming this new firm, one paramount characteristic stood out: the complete absence of personal greed. That does not mean that we are not ambitious or that we do not want to be successful and earn good money. However, we define success in ways beyond just the amount of money we individually earn.

Leadership Thought and Application

Though the structure of law firms and other organizations that provide traditional legal services may change in the future, leadership at its core will not change. The means and tools that leaders use may change, but true leadership and the principles of gaining positive influence over the lives of others will never change. That said, it is important for every leader to understand how changes in organizational structure and technology will change the ways leaders motivate and influence followers.

New management and leadership structures. More nonlawyer professionals are likely to appear in all levels of law firm management and administration. The profession has already seen a slow progression from bookkeeper to COO, and the profession can expect a similar progression toward nonlawyer executive leadership—a chief executive officer—even in traditional firms. The law firm as a professional service provider will be seen more as a business, and lawyer leaders will need to adapt to this new view. They must realize that general business and leadership principles apply just as much to law firms and other professions as they do to any business organization. Members of the firm must realize that professionals who are hired for their business expertise are capable of making good (and in many cases better) business decisions for law firms.

The effects of virtual practice. Both management and leadership will continue to change as the amount of face-to-face meeting time between lawyers, and between lawyers and their clients, continues to decline. This trend has grown over the past fifteen years, as the volume of communication has shifted from phone calls and letters to e-mail. Although e-mail is electronic, it is similar to letters and written memos. In the future, collaborative tools that use the Internet will be more common both for internal communications and correspondence between legal service providers and consumers. The telephone as a means of voice communication may give way to tools such as video conferencing and applications such as iPad's Facetime. Lawyers and clients will use these tools and so will law firm leaders and their members who are separated by geography. Most likely they will also be used for interfirm communication between offices in one building or between lawyers in an office and those who are working at home. Leaders of law firms and legal organizations will need to understand that different forms of communication require different leadership skills. Service and influence as a leader will still be the key to leadership, but it must be achieved using new tools and techniques. The job of the leader is to stay abreast of and adapt to changes in technology.

Changing expectations. The Morningstar Law Group illustrates a trend: some lawyers are not looking for life in a traditional law firm. In the past fifteen to twenty years, more new law graduates have sought employers with nontraditional value systems. These lawyers are less likely to be interested in ownership of the firm through traditional partnership status. And this values shift seems to have caught on with the middle generation of lawyers as well. Some lawyers who have attained partnership status after years at a law firm now find that partnership is not all that it was cracked up to be. They are asking themselves if something better is out there. Leaders must truly understand the changing values of all firm members. Part of the role of a law firm leader is to establish values that will be shared by members of the firm. If a leader is not in tune with the values of individual firm members, his or her ability to positively influence others' action will be drastically hampered or even impossible. As an example, if law firm managers are disappointed with partners' financial performance and want to institute an accountability system, they must understand partners' values: which do they value more, financial performance or individual autonomy? Law firm leaders need that answer before developing policies and procedures. Leaders can no longer assume that the professional values of the 1980s still apply today.

Consumers' changing demands. The Novus and Axiom examples indicate that clients are no longer willing to put up with business as usual. New ways of providing legal services are being created every year, and most of these methods either take business away from traditional law firms or drive down the fees that can be charged. Therefore, leaders of lawyers must take the lead in managing client relationships. Leaders need to help firm members understand the client's perception of value: how the relationship is maintained and how the firm's services are different from lower-priced alternatives. The number of billable hours on a client matter is no longer the key feature of the relationship.

As a final comment, as stated elsewhere, lawyers and law firms are not exempt from changes in leadership thought and concepts that uniformly apply to other businesses and professional services organizations. If you are interested in keeping up with leadership trends and concepts generally, check out Bob Johansen's **Institute for the Future** website (www.iftf.org).

Questions to Ponder

- Do you or the members of your law firm have the view that changes in the profession, such as the examples described in

this chapter, are not likely to affect your law firm? What is the reason for this conclusion?
- Do you find that changes in communication over the past several years have made leadership more difficult? In what ways? What specific actions can you, as a leader of a law firm, take to counter the difficulties of leadership presented by the increase of virtual practice?
- Have you been able to lead your firm in differentiating your services from those provided by lower-cost alternatives? If so, how? If not, what steps can you take to do so? How can you help members provide quality legal service and help clients understand the need for the quality your firm provides? What steps can you take to help educate others in your firm about the changing definition of *quality service* and how clients may define that term?

Suggested Reading
Frances Hesselbein and Marshall Goldsmith, eds., *The Leader of the Future 2* (San Francisco: Jossey-Bass, 2006).

Patrick McKenna and Brian K. Burke, *Serving at the Pleasure of My Partners: Advice to the New Firm Leader* (Danvers, MA: Thomson Reuters, 2011).

Chapter 3
DEVELOPMENT OF PERSONAL LEADERSHIP SKILLS

> [T]he real opportunity for success lies within the person and not the job . . . you can best get to the top by getting to the bottom of things . . . success and happiness are not matters of chance but choice.
>
> —Zig Ziglar[20]

All law firms need strong and effective leadership. Leadership is not, however, something anyone is just born with. It is developed over many years. Law firms in particular have unique management and leadership needs. Many of these needs are due to law firms' (and other professional service firms') organizational structure, which is not a typical pyramid. Regardless of this fact, at the core leadership is the same, and those in positions of authority who desire to be effective need to dedicate themselves to developing leadership skills. Simply put, this requires effort, discipline, and sacrifice. A leader who stays focused on skills development and maintains a balanced life will not only achieve success, but will find the role genuinely fulfilling.

Suggested Reading
Zig Ziglar, *See You at the Top* (Los Angeles: Pelican Publishing, 1979).
Laurie Beth Jones, *Jesus: Life Coach* (New York: MFJ Books, 2004).

---

20. *See You at the Top*, page 24.

Discipline 1
Passion and Focus

Passion is a product of the heart. Passion is what helps you when you have a great dream. Passion breeds conviction and turns mediocrity into excellence! Your passion will motivate others to join you in pursuit of your dream. With passion, you will overcome insurmountable obstacles. You will become unstoppable! . . . And now I have made a decision with my heart. I am not timid. I will move now and not look back. . . . I will not wait. I am passionate about my vision for the future. My course has been charted. My destiny is assured. I have a decided heart.

—Andy Andrews[21]

Before attending law school, my vision (my physical eyesight) was always measured at 20/20. About midway through my second year, my long-range vision started to get blurry. By the time I received my law degree a little over a year later, I was wearing the stylish horn-rimmed glasses popular in the 1980s. My glasses actually started with a very thin glass width, but my eyesight continued to worsen until my lenses looked like the bottom of a Coke bottle just a few years later. I have now transitioned to what are known as graduated, or progressive, lenses. For someone who is nearsighted, this type of lens is graduated so that the bottom of the lens allows for viewing things up close and the top of the lens is more powerful for

---

21. Andy Andrews, *The Traveler's Gift* (Nashville: Thomas Nelson, 2002), pages 81 and 89.

long-distance viewing. For me, the lenses were a little difficult to get used to at first; however, I have now simply grown accustomed to being able to focus, at all times, on things both near and far.

In a much different way, law firm leaders must also desire to be continually focused. It must be like the focus permitted with graduated lenses. A singular focus on the short term can result in firm management attending to the many very difficult problems that arise on a daily basis but may also have the undesired consequence of the leader not being in a position to give direction to followers in the future. A singular focus on the long term, without at least an appropriate and effective delegation of day-to-day management to qualified administrative professionals, can result in disasters, which delay or divert long-range plans.

The first discipline of a law firm leader is passion and focus. A leader can have passion without focus; however, it is very hard to be truly focused in your leadership unless you have passion for what you are focused on. The lessons within this chapter will look at a few activities that should help every law firm leader maintain appropriate focus. Doing so, leaders will find that the passion they have for the success of their law firms will more likely be put to good use.

First, before a leader can help any group of followers determine where they individually and collectively want to go, he or she must have an understanding of reality: a true and realistic definition of both individual and firm-wide present reality. Whether a new leader is just starting out or has been a member of management for a long time, there are some things that can be done to be kept abreast of what shape the firm is truly in.

Next, law firm leadership can be a very lonely place, and those in leadership roles need to understand the importance of being surrounded by others who are qualified to be mentors and coaches in leadership concepts, skills, and struggles.

Finally, every leader needs to be constantly immersed in leadership education. Leadership principles are not that difficult to understand, but without regular and diverse study, these basic principles will be most difficult to recall and apply at those crucial times when they are needed the most.

LESSON 8 DEFINE REALITY

The main thing is to keep the main thing the main thing.

—Stephen R. Covey[22]

You really do have to know where you are before you can figure out where you are headed or where you want to lead others. If a leader doesn't understand his or her current situation and the current facts about the firm, however brutal they may be, it will be difficult to take the firm anywhere. The reality of the firm is not necessarily what firm members think it is or what clients say it is. It may not even be what firm leaders tell each other it is. And finally, just because firm owners have agreed on a mission statement or a strategic plan doesn't make it a reality either. Unfortunately for many law firms, reality isn't clear until the organization is faced with a difficult situation or crisis; for example, when an entire practice group departs or when finances require massive layoffs of associates.

I was amazed to hear members of one midsize East Coast firm say what a great culture they had. They clearly believe that their firm is a much better place to work than other firms in their small city. In fact, they describe their competitors as unpleasant places to work. From my observation, the members of this law firm do not really understand their own culture. They pride themselves on collegiality. At the same time, I saw little or no accountability or teamwork in the substantive work that they perform or the administrative roles they have committed to. The compensation system includes a bonus program that is mostly "eat-what-you-kill." Members have little incentive to chip in and take care of the business side of the law practice, such as management, marketing, finance, and technology. Even with their bonus system, some lawyers are clearly overpaid considering both objective standards and other members'

---

22. *First Things First*, page 75.

perceptions of value. When members of the firm give notice and leave, there is no real exit interview that asks about the reasons for the departure. Other members generally blame the departure on some shortcoming of the person who is leaving—why he or she did not fit into the culture and needed to leave. The members of the executive committee say that leading the membership anywhere is very difficult, but they do not accurately define where the firm truly is at the present time. Instead they fool themselves with a definition of reality that is a myth.

Leadership Thought and Application

Max Depree, leadership guru, former CEO of Herman Miller, and best-selling author, writes: "The first responsibility of a leader is to define reality. The last is to say thank you. In between the two, the leader must become a servant and a debtor."[23] This lesson is focused on the first responsibility Depree expresses. What does it mean to define reality, and how does a leader do it?

Other leadership experts have confirmed the need to define reality:

> The art of managing and leading comes down to a simple thing. Determining and facing reality about people, situations, products, and then acting decisively and quickly on that reality. Think how many times we have procrastinated, hoped it would get better. Most of the mistakes you've made have been through not being willing to face into it, straight in the mirror that reality you find, then taking action on it. That's all managing is, defining and acting. Not hoping, not waiting for the next plan. Not rethinking it. Getting on with it. Doing it. Defining and doing it.
>
> —Jack Welch, former General Electric CEO[24]

---

23. Max Depree, *Leadership Is an Art* (New York: Doubleday, 2004), page 11.
24. Quoted in "Thoughts on Real*ity* Thinking: Quotes," Reality Thinking!, accessed May 18, 2013, www.realitythinking.com/quotes.html.

> Designing and implementing a strategy for change is a waste of time until you have discovered and embraced the current reality. If you don't know where you really are, it is impossible to get where you need to be. What you don't know can kill you.
>
> —Andy Stanley[25]

> Realism is the heart of execution, but many organizations are full of people who are trying to avoid or shade reality. Why? It makes life uncomfortable. People don't want to open Pandora's box . . . Sometimes the leaders are simply in denial. When we ask leaders to describe their organization's strengths and weaknesses, they generally state the strengths fairly well, but they're not so good on identifying the weaknesses.
>
> —Larry Bossidy and Ram Charan[26]

> You absolutely cannot make a series of good decisions without first confronting the brutal facts . . . The good to great companies continually refined the path to greatness with the brutal facts of the reality.
>
> —Jim Collins[27]

Leaders need to be realists; otherwise members will not follow them on a quest to achieve goals that seem unrealistic.

Josh Lowry's blog *CustomerThink* (www.customerthink.com) further explores the topic:

> In his book *Straight from the Gut* (Warner Business Books, 2001), Jack Welch, the former Chairman and CEO of General Electric (1981-2001), outlined six rules for successful leadership. Of the six rules, five involved defining/facing reality. Welch's six rules were:
>
> 1. Be candid with everyone.

---

25. Andy Stanley, *The Next Generation Leader* (Sisters, OR: Multnomah, 2003), page 73.
26. Larry Bossidy and Ram Charan, *Execution: The Discipline of Getting Things Done* (New York: Random House, 2002), page 67.
27. Jim Collins, *Good to Great* (New York: Harper Collins, 2001), pages 70–71.

2. Change before you have to.
3. Control your destiny or someone else will.
4. Do not manage, lead.
5. Face reality as it is, not as it was or as you wish it were.
6. If you do not have a competitive advantage, do not compete.

These rules along with the following ideas will help you uncover the realities—the brutal facts—in your law firm:

Know the background information of your firm. To know a law firm well, a leader must know not only the objective facts of the organization but also the truths about the communities that the firm is a part of. It is critical to understand the operating norms of the legal services industry and the state and local bars. It is just as important to understand the business communities in which the firm operates, including how they change and how those changes could affect the firm. A leader must be well-informed about the firm's capabilities and the financial status of its assets. It is important to measure the firm with key performance indicators, such as hours worked, new matters opened, partner hours to total hours, charge-off percentages, and the ratio of unbilled work to average fee billings. A leader needs this data provided in a form that he or she can gauge individual and practice group performance as well as firm performance.

Inquire of your people. After a leader has gathered the facts, he or she needs to know how members from all levels of the firm see the firm's present reality. Firm members need an opportunity to express how they see the firm's present reality and to articulate their ideas and concerns about the firm. Though the opinions of firm members are not conclusive, a leader needs to understand the opinions and examine the reasons behind each opinion. Ask questions such as the following:

1. What works in our law firm? What does not?
2. What holds us back?

3. What are your likes and dislikes about our firm and the way it is run, managed, led?
4. What motivates you? What makes you happy?
5. How do you see the future of the firm?
6. Do you feel empowered by policies or held back by them?

Tell the truth. After a leader has gathered the objective and subjective facts, he or she needs to consolidate the information and come to conclusions. What did the leader discover, and what conclusions need to be shared with firm members? Firm stakeholders need to have answers to the following questions, even if it means sharing difficult information:

1. Where are we?
2. Where are we headed, or where do we need to be headed?
3. What challenges will we encounter as we alter our present course?
4. What obstacles and pitfalls will we come up against if we do not change?

If leaders fail to discover, reveal, and address the brutal facts, members of the firm live in fear of the future and the unknown.

Personal leadership development. The same process and questions used to determine a law firm's reality apply equally to the personal development of a lawyer as a leader. Each of the above principles can, and should, be applied by the leader to his or her personal growth. Questions regarding knowledge of personal reality, the brutal facts as applied to individual leadership effectiveness, and how a leader is doing in his or her role need to be examined on a regular basis. The outline above can easily be applied for this purpose.

Questions to Ponder

- What are the quiet truths in your organization—things that everyone knows and no one wants to talk about or address—that are preventing the firm from achieving its mission?
- Is it difficult to confront members with reality? Do you have difficulty accurately describing reality to firm members? Why? What can you do to institute more positive, constructive "truth telling" among your ownership group?
- Have you applied the reality principles and the brutal fact tests of this lesson to your personal life and leadership? What brutal facts of your own leadership do you need to face? Write down three or four of them. Looking at the list, what can you commit to do to change them?

Suggested Reading

Stephen R. Covey, *First Things First* (New York: Simon & Schuster, 1994).

Stephen M. R. Covey, *The Speed of Trust* (New York: Simon & Schuster, 2006).

Henry Cloud, Integrity: The Courage to Meet the Demands of Reality (New York: Harper Collins, 2006)

LESSON 9 COACHES AND MENTORS

To be the next generation leader you can be, you must enlist the help of others. Self-evaluation is helpful, but evaluation from someone else is essential. You need a leadership coach.

—Andy Stanley[28]

Consider the progression of life. At some point, usually between grade school and high school, most children determine that they "know it all" and consequently no longer take kindly to advice from parents or other adults who have gained experience and wisdom over many years. For most children, this phase passes, and later they realize that they really do not know it all. However, some individuals cling to this belief and therefore stop learning. As detailed throughout this book, leaders can use many tools to learn how to more effectively influence those they have the privilege to serve, including studying books, attending conferences, watching videos and listening to recorded seminars. This chapter describes leadership education through relationships and the experiences of others.

My firm has experience with coaches. Over the years, several of our lawyers have had professional coaching. Coaches have helped correct shortcomings and refine expertise. We have found that having a coach need not, and should not, be seen as a stigma, but a valuable professional development tool. It has also been our experience that resistance to coaching is generally due to a stereotype created in the learner's mind.

In my experience as a firm leader, I have had both coaches and mentors. Leadership coaches are generally more effective when they can observe the leader at work. My coaches were elder lawyers who had led my firm in the past and present. They are people whom I highly respect and who are quite knowledgeable and experienced in

---
28. *The Next Generation Leader*, page 106.

law firm management and leadership. I could ask my coaches about issues of law firm leadership and management, and they were close enough to the firm that they could observe and critique my activities.

In addition to the coaches, I have been fortunate that very experienced and accomplished businesspeople are willing to meet with me on a regular basis. These people have excelled in leadership in their own lives, and they are willing to be my sounding boards for difficult issues—usually interpersonal—that arise from time to time. In addition, they regularly challenge me in areas of personal development and growth. These few devoted friends are my mentors.

Leadership Thought and Application

In *The Lawyer's Guide to Professional Coaching*, Andrew Elowitt defines coaching as "a professional service that helps a person (or group of people) enhance or improve their performance, experience, satisfaction, clarity, or circumstances."[29] Mentoring is more about personal guidance in one-on-one dialogue. It is a relationship that leads to learning and action. Every law firm leader should consider both of these coaching and mentoring relationships as tools to develop leadership skills and to contribute to professional, and personal development.

Firm leader. For a firm leader, the coaching relationship is more about having a sounding board and receiving advice based on experience. A coach may have personal experience in a role similar to the leader's, but if not, the coach usually has experience helping or observing others in the same or a very similar role. Many lists set forth the characteristics of a good coach. However, the leader of a law firm is in a special position because partners often believe they should have just as much say about an issue as the managing partner, practice group leaders, or members of the management

---

29. Andrew Elowitt, *The Lawyer's Guide to Professional Coaching* (Chicago: American Bar Association, 2012), page xxiii.

committee. To help address these special issues, some qualities are more important than others. Consider these few very important characteristics of a good law firm leadership coach:

1. **Listens.** An extremely critical aspect of any coaching relationship is the ability and desire to listen. A coaching relationship includes regular verbal communication, but a coach must go beyond simply hearing to actively listening to the leader. A coach who does not listen cannot teach, direct, or hold accountable.

2. **Is learned and can facilitate learning.** A good coach needs to help a leader learn and understand things that cannot be learned from a book or a recording. This type of learning comes from experience and is ideally related to the practical aspects of law firm leadership. For example, a former managing partner of the leader's firm might be a good coach for a newer managing partner.

3. **Is respected in the profession.** Clearly if the coach is a former managing partner or member of the firm, the leader will know whether the coach is respected. Professional respect indicates that the coach has the knowledge and experience to provide valuable coaching. Some consultants provide coaching services specifically to lawyers. Some of them are highly skilled in coaching, and others have just added coaching as one more service they provide as well-rounded law firm consultants. If you are considering making a financial commitment to a professional coach, choose one experienced in law firm leadership. You will need to do your homework to make sure that the one you are considering has the requisite knowledge and experience and is well respected in the profession.

4. **Sets goals and holds accountable.** A coaching relationship does not exist so the leader can have a sounding board or friend. The coach needs to use knowledge and experience,

along with active listening, to help the leader develop personal missions and goals. Then the coach needs to meet regularly with the leader and hold him or her accountable for achieving goals, and in the event of failures, help the leader avoid repeating the mistakes and failures.

The relationship with a mentor is a little different. It is less about achieving management and leadership goals and strategies and more about achieving success in life generally. For example, issues a leader might regularly discuss with a mentor may include the difficulties of balancing leadership, work, family, and other activities. Consider these few very important characteristics of a good mentor:

1. **Listens.** In the same way and for the same reasons as a coach, a good mentor is a good listener.
2. **Asks probing questions.** A mentor must be able to dig deep when questioning the protégé. Investigating reasons for the leader's positions, actions, and decisions of the leader and examining and discussing motives are a mentor's responsibility.
3. **Provides constructive practical feedback.** A mentor must be insightful and analytical. To repeat, the relationship is not that of friend or sounding board. The mentor should challenge the leader and provide constructive and—when necessary—blunt feedback. A mentor with well-rounded or vast life experiences is more able to listen, probe, and give useful feedback. For example, good mentors will often be able to share stories as examples for the leader to consider.
4. **Offers hope, optimism, and support.** Because a leader chooses to share his or her life experiences, it is extremely important for the mentor to have a generally positive attitude about life and about the leader's life, career, and future. A leader must choose a mentor wisely. When asking someone to serve in this role, be careful that the mentor truly

wants to serve. Even an experienced person is not a good mentor if he or she is just "doing you a favor."

Firm members. Both coaching and mentoring relationships can be very valuable for all firm members. It is the firm leader's job to help followers understand the value of these relationships when it appears that members could benefit from professional or personal guidance. Identifying a need early can prevent it from building into a crisis. When the need is related to a specific area of practice, the leader may recommend a coach. Issues that could benefit from coaching include, for example, time management for balancing a significant caseload; ineffective client communications; and time, billing, and other administrative organizational issues. Some law firms have formal programs that are called mentor programs, but they function much more like coaching relationships. In these programs a younger associate is teamed up with a more experienced or seasoned lawyer, who provides sage advice about specific practice-related issues. These established programs are great examples of coaching because their purpose is to avoid problems and develop professional skills.

When a member of the firm has a broader professional issue, a qualified mentor might be a good choice. For example, a firm leader may suggest a mentoring relationship for an associate who does not appear to be a good fit for private practice or for a long-term partner who seems to be going through a midlife crisis. For problems such as these, a leader may also recommend more experienced professional help from a psychologist or counselor. However, a mentor relationship is not only for problems. A relationship with a trusted advisor can help any member of the firm examine personal goals and life vision and understand the relationship between those goals and the law firm's mission and purpose. Leaders may hesitate to encourage such relationships because they could cause a productive and efficient lawyer to change the focus of his or her personal life. However, the overall success and happiness of followers (what one might call service to those led) should be a leader's most important focus. In the long run an organization that puts its members' interests first will succeed.

Ground rules for an effective coach or mentor relationship. In addition to the above specific considerations for selecting a mentor or coach, the following characteristics of a good relationship should also be considered:

1. Agreement that the content of discussions is private or secret
2. Commitment to meet regularly
3. Accountability
4. Open and honest communication—a commitment to not put on airs
5. No direct stake in the outcome of the relationship for the mentor or coach
6. Trust in the relationship
7. No need to impress each other

For a more detailed and in-depth consideration of the use of coaching for professional development of your firm members, refer to *The Lawyer's Guide to Professional Coaching*, by Andrew Elowitt.

Questions to Ponder

- Do you have a mentor or coach relationship for your own leadership? If not, do you feel one could be beneficial to you?
- Have there been issues in your firm where a mentoring or coaching relationship could have avoided a larger problem? What did you learn from that experience? Have you put in place any plan based on that experience?
- Does your firm have an established mentor program? Are the right people appointed as mentors, or are mentors chosen

based on a seniority system or some other basis that does not necessarily consider the needs of the member and strengths of the mentor? What type of system could you as a leader set up to identify the correct people to serve as mentors and coaches for your firm members?

Suggested Reading

Andy Stanley, *The Next Generation Leader* (Sisters, OR: Multnomah, 2003).

John C. Maxwell, *Your Road Map for Success* (Nashville: Thomas Nelson, 2002).

Andrew Elowitt, *The Lawyer's Guide to Professional Coaching* (Chicago: American Bar Association, 2012).

LESSON 10 EDUCATION PLAN

Personal growth is essential to good leadership. Far from thinking he has attained, the effective leader is continually seeking to learn from his experiences and become more efficient in his work.

—Hudson T. Armerding[30]

I have attended many leadership conferences over the past twelve years. A question arises at almost every one: Is anyone born a good leader? Invariably, the answer is no. Certainly some individuals have special gifts that make them more likely to excel as leaders. For some people, however, leadership skills are not revealed until there is a crisis or life-changing event.

At the 2012 American Bar Association annual meeting, Morris Dees received the highest honor the association bestows on any lawyer, the ABA Medal. Dees received this medal for his years of dedicated and selfless service combating racism and the Ku Klux Klan. His long-standing leadership is unquestioned. By his personal account, however, Dees was not a born leader. His biography on the Southern Poverty Law Center website describes an ambitious young man with a highly profitable business and a very successful legal career. The biography suggests that Dees learned many leadership principles, but initially he applied them for his own gain and interests. After a trial in which he had represented a KKK member, Dees had a conversation with an African American. As a result, he began to think about where his life was headed. Later, after the KKK set fire to many African American churches, Dees pleaded to his own church to help these churches. Being rebuffed in his pleas, Dees moved ahead without his church, and it is at this point his understanding of servant leadership became evident. Dees's life became an

---

30. *Leadership*, page 154.

example of service to and leadership of others, many of whom were incapable of leading themselves because of their circumstances. At the Southern Poverty Law Center's website (www.splcenter.org), you can read more about Dees's life after he sold his business so he could lead a civil rights law practice.

An example from another era also illustrates the need to learn leadership skills. Teedie was a sickly child who suffered from severe asthma and frequent body aches and stomach pains. His parents tried the numerous treatments doctors prescribed, but nothing remedied his ailments. As a result Teedie often remained inside and rarely associated with other children in the neighborhood. His confinement likely prompted his lifelong practice of daily journal writing. Teedie's father often read aloud to his son, and Teedie began reading all types of books. Eventually Teedie's asthma disappeared, and he made a concerted effort to overcome all of his weaknesses, including his weakness of body. For the rest of his life, Teedie, Theodore Roosevelt, was committed to learning. Roosevelt understood that a leader must always continue to self-educate: "As soon as any man has ceased to be able to learn, his usefulness as a teacher is at an end. When he himself can't learn, he has reached the stage where other people can't learn from him."[31]

Leadership Thought and Application

You cannot hope or wish your way into being a good leader. Effective leadership requires hard work and determination. Leadership skills can be learned in a variety of ways—through reading books or watching videos, or from observation and hands-on experience. There are many ways people can learn to be good leaders. If you are not sure which method will be most effective for you, choose a variety of learning tools. Learning to be a leader is much different from learning a

---

31. James M. Strock, *Theodore Roosevelt on Leadership: Lessons from the Bully Pulpit*, page 62.

technically complex subject like rocket science. Leadership principles are not tough to understand. They are, however, extremely difficult to implement in real-life situations. Almost everyday a typical leader encounters situations that call for immediate action, action that requires exemplary leadership for the good of the organization and its people. Though leadership principles are easy to understand, they can be difficult to remember in the heat of the moment. However, a well-rounded education that immerses you in principles of leadership concepts and provides examples of their successful application will help you recall the principles when you really need them. Here are some basic leadership tools to consider:

1. **Self education.** The positive aspect of self-learning is that the materials (books, CDs, leadership club resources, blogs, and videos) have a relatively low monetary cost, or they may even be free. The negative aspect is that self-learning requires discipline, a commitment to prioritize the long-term ahead of the immediate. Day-to-day issues will arise, and at the time they will seem much more important than studying leadership. The student must resist these distractions.

   Many kinds of leadership books are available. Most of them (such as books by John Maxwell, Ken Blanchard, Jim Kouzes, and Barry Posner) are written in the first person and describe specific applications of leadership principles. Other books (for example, those by Patrick Lencioni and Andy Andrews) use parables to show how concepts might apply in a typical situation. Books about U.S. presidents or about world leaders, such as Churchill, Mandela, or Ghandi, also illustrate leadership principles. Leadership clubs (the Maximum Impact Club is an example) also offer self-education. For a nominal membership fee, you will receive a monthly leadership resource, such as a newsletter, magazine, or CD. An advantage of a CD is that you can learn while you are driving (but remember to also keep your attention on the road). The web has many general and law firm leadership blogs you can read (for example, try www.johnmaxwellonleadership.com, http://www.tablegroup.com/pat/povs/, or http://www.leadership-forlawyers.typepad.com/). Excellent videos are available at www.ted.com. Each video is no longer than twenty minutes and offers a great break from billable work.

2. **Seminars and events.** A seminar or event requires the leader's commitment to leave the office, turn off e-mail, and, for at least a short period of time, be immersed in leadership education. (I consider non-interactive web based events where you are located in your own office to be self-learning.) There are many local and national events, and many of the national events conduct simulcasts throughout the country. One of the best is Leadercast (www.giantimpact.com), which is held annually in Atlanta, Georgia, and also broadcast live throughout the country to central locations.

3. **Program of study.** A variety of academic programs have popped up all over the country, and many are tied to universities or law schools. Some programs are more formal and require a commitment similar to law school. Others are online graduate-level courses, and still others require a relatively short-term commitment and have no examinations. One of the oldest established programs is at George Washington University School of Law. Other organizations, such as the Center for Creative Leadership (www.ccl.org), also offer leadership development courses. Some of the organizations are non-profit, and the structure of the courses may vary from traditional classroom instruction to online self-paced programs to programs that emphasize experiential learning. Some programs can be customized for the learner's needs. For example, a coach may observe a leader in action and provide direct one-to-one feedback.

4. **Direct meetings and interviews.** One of the best ways to learn about leadership is by meeting with known leaders and asking them questions. You can be bold and try to meet with nationally known leadership speakers and teachers. However, every leader almost certainly knows one or two exemplary leaders. It may be a college or law school professor, a politician, the head of a community organization, a religious leader, or perhaps someone in your church or synagogue who has recently retired from a position of leadership in the secular world. Ask these types of folks out for lunch (on you) and see if they are willing to answer questions about their successes and challenges as leaders through the years. Most true leaders—those who have servant hearts—will be more than glad to spend a few minutes helping you learn about leadership.

Questions to Ponder

- Are there any people that you know who seem to fit the term *natural born leader*? What gives you this impression? Are you certain the skills are innate, or have they been developed over time?
- What types of leadership education materials most appeal to you? Have you set aside a specific amount of time to develop and refine your leadership skills? If not, what is the one thing that keeps you from doing so, and what can be done about this obstacle?
- Can you identify any great leaders whom you already know? Who are they? What qualities do you see in them that make them great? Can you learn from any of them? Commit to asking one such leader to have lunch with you every month for six months.

Suggested Reading

Hudson T. Armerding, *Leadership* (Wheaton, IL: Tyndale House 1978).

James M. Strock, *Theodore Roosevelt on Leadership: Lessons from the Bully Pulpit* (New York: Three Rivers Press, 2001).

Discipline 2

Balance

Calmness of mind is one of the beautiful jewels of wisdom. It is the result of long and patient effort in self-control. Its presence is an indication of ripened experience, and of a more than ordinary knowledge of the laws and operations of thought.... The more tranquil a man becomes, the greater is his success, his influence, his power for good.

— James Allen[32]

Each year before my annual physical, I go on the South Beach Diet. I can usually lose fifteen to twenty pounds in two weeks when I am on that diet. My theory is that if I'm on the diet and my blood sugar or other numbers are totally "out of whack," I will know I have a problem. If I'm not on the diet and one of my numbers is slightly out of range, my physician will ask me to make all types of drastic lifestyle changes, even though the number that's out of whack may be a result of something as inconsequential as a mere cup of coffee. Some of my friends think this is ridiculous. Deep down I imagine I know they are right. It is better to have a well-rounded and balanced lifestyle all the time: one that includes a balanced diet, stress control, regular physical activity, moderate alcohol intake, and no smoking.

In the same way, a leader who desires well-developed and effective leadership skills must have a balanced lifestyle both in and out of the office. Obviously, problems with physical health can interfere

---
32. *As a Man Thinketh* (New York: Grossett & Dunlap, 1974), pages 69–70.

with a leader's ability to perform. This chapter discusses a few special activities that are directly related to a leader's balance of life and work and his or her ability to perform as a leader:

1. **Time management.** Effective use of the most limited of resources: time.

2. **Communication.** Implementation of proper communication principles and individual policies and rules to assure that communication protects and enhances followers' trust in the leader.

3. **Alone time.** Scheduling a regular block of time for studying leadership and contemplating long-term issues.

4. **Time off.** Understanding that all work and no play not only makes for a dull life but may also make for a less effective leader.

5. **Strengths and weaknesses.** Knowing the importance of building up your strengths, and surrounding yourself with people whose strengths are in the areas of your weakness.

LESSON 11 TIME MANAGEMENT

Psalm 23, Antithesis
The Clock is my dictator, I shall not rest.
It makes me lie down only when exhausted.
It leads me to deep depression, it hounds my soul.
It leads me in circles of frenzy for activities' sake.
Even though I run frantically from task to task,
I will never get it all done, for my "ideal" is with me.
Deadlines and my need for approval, they drive me.
They demand performance from me, beyond the limits of my schedule.
They anoint my head with migraines, my in-basket overflows.
Surely fatigue and time pressure shall follow me all the days of my life,
And I will dwell in the bonds of frustration forever.

—Marcia Hornok[33]

As a leader of several different organizations and through my observations of other law firms, I have encountered many examples of poor time management. Often I have heard that an individual is a procrastinator. That may be true, but how useful is such a factual, results-oriented conclusion based on a typical definition of *procrastination?* Here are some typical law firm scenarios I have either observed or heard of:

1. **Inability or unwillingness to prioritize.** The person (lawyer, staff member, or administrator) makes a typical to-do list, but the list is not prioritized. Items are added to the list as they arise. Items are pulled off of the list in a priority that seems based on the individual's preferences:

---

33. Marcia Hornok, "Psalm 23, Antithesis," originally published in *Discipleship Journal* 60 (November/December 1990).

enjoyable activities are done first. Sometimes prioritizing actions based on the firm's best interest yields one order, and prioritizing actions to meet clients' best interests results in a different order. In this case, setting priorities can be extremely difficult, and the result may look like procrastination. It may appear that the leader is procrastinating when the firm's interests dictate one order of priorities and the clients' interests dictate another.

2. **Lack of focus.** The person may arrive on time and may often stay late. The day starts with a cup of coffee, some chit chat (which, because people are too polite to tell the person to go away, also reduces *their* productivity), followed by checking e-mail and a few popular political, sports, or other Internet sites. Then the person attempts to work, but interruptions such as e-mail alarms prevent him or her from getting much done before lunch, which might run up to an hour or an hour and half. Productivity, or lack thereof, remains constant in the afternoon, as the firm member is still unable to focus and uses any interruption as an excuse to waste his or her own time or the time of others. By quitting time, much work is left for the evening or next day, and deadlines may be missed.

3. **An inability to say no.** The problem may not be prioritizing work but an inability to refuse a request. The to-do list quickly becomes unmanageable, and the lawyer either looks or is disorganized, inefficient, or unprofessional. Unreturned phone calls, a constantly full voice messaging system, late billing, and missed deadlines can be consequences of not saying no.

4. **Not delegating.** A lawyer with a full workload may turn work away directly or, by appearing too busy, turn it away indirectly. Instead of delegating work, the lawyer often complains that he or she has no time to delegate or supervise. (I

know this from experience because I have struggled with delegating.)

5. **Late billing.** Some lawyers never seem to have the time to record their time. Failures in daily record keeping lead to delays in monthly bills being sent to clients. Clients have often moved on to other issues and may forget the positive work the lawyer did on their behalf. Beyond time management concerns, lawyers need to be aware that, absent perfect recall, it is unethical to reconstruct billable time at the end of the month.

6. **Personal distractions.** Staff members who spend too much time using the Internet for personal business or engage in interoffice gossip or general conversation may not get their work done on time. In addition, they are less available to help others on the team meet common organizational goals.

7. **Lack of confidence.** If associates or partners working on a client matter are not confident in their legal ability, they may be afraid to finish. In the words of a former managing partner of my firm, the lawyer needs to be told, "Stop stewing and start doing." Obviously, lack of confidence can be caused by many factors.

Procrastination certainly has many causes. For instance, a member may fail to understand and be a part of the firm's mission and vision. The cause may be outside of work, such as a personal life crisis or substance abuse; however, in my experience procrastination commonly results from poor time management.

Leadership Thought and Application

For some consultants the term *time management* is a popular buzzword. Other consultants do not identify time management as a concept that will make a person more effective. In his book *First Things First*, the late Stephen R. Covey differentiates his concepts from traditional time management, saying that time management is about efficiency, and his concepts are life principles. I love the writings of Mr. Covey, but my read of his very helpful book is that it is another quite effective way of tackling the broad concept of time management.

Every member of a law firm needs to wisely manage the time spent practicing law. Regardless of their leadership responsibilities, all lawyers and other members of the firm need to balance their time so that they perform all of their duties, whether billable or nonbillable. For leaders who are also responsible for billable work (such as a managing partner or a lawyer member of a management committee), time management is even more critical. Firm members expect leaders to follow uniform policies and meet a billable expectation, and they also look to leaders for guidance and direction.

"Busyness" almost always leads to a more stressful life. Being busy, however, does not necessarily mean being effective. These tips can help provide greater balance, focus, and effectiveness when combining a substantive practice with a management and leadership role:

1. Don't be guided by circumstances but instead by your mission and that of the law firm. You may need to recognize that someone else's emergency is not your emergency. Obviously, you must consider client work and emergencies in light of your obligations under the Rules of Professional Conduct. However, assuming compliance with those standards, law firm leaders and leaders of client matters would do well to consider this basic principle.

2. Don't let the loudest, most difficult, or pushiest voice in the firm get you off track. Leaders and team members are responsible for advancing the mission and vision of the firm and communicating this mission and vision to the other members of the firm or team. This responsibility sometimes requires that you not cave in to the most insistent voice in the group.

3. A stop-doing list is a key to time management. My friend and expert consultant Gerry Riskin, of Edge International, says that every lawyer, each year, should "fire" 5 to 10 percent of their clients. A stop-doing list follows the same basic idea. The theory is that a lawyer leader's effectiveness increases when he or she gets rid of clients and activities that consume the most resources, but do not provide the most productivity or satisfaction. In many cases a majority of a leader's emotional and time resources are consumed by a very small percentage of the client base or management issues. Getting rid of these large consumers may increase productivity, accomplishment, and success.

4. All firm members should set aside a specific time for the most important activities. For leaders, those include touchy-feely activities as well as managing day-to-day tasks. Because many leaders are less familiar or comfortable with the relational parts of the role, they are reluctant to find time for them. As a result, leaders need to devote time in their schedules to learn and perform these tasks until they become second nature. Leaders with strong interpersonal skills may need to schedule time for some other important but personally uncomfortable aspect of their position.

Questions to Ponder

- In viewing all of the different hats that you wear in the law firm, are there any that you do not wear well? Which ones? Why are they challenging? Do you need to schedule a time in your day, week, or month to specifically address these areas?
- Do you have any loud or pushy voices in your law firm that get you off track? To what extent have you been able to move forward even so? What actions do you need to take to assure these voices do not hinder the firm from achieving its vision?

- Can you identify any things that should be on a stop-doing list? Do any of your followers need a stop-doing list? What plan can your firm's leadership team implement to encourage others in the firm to have a stop-doing list?

Suggested Reading

Todd Duncan, *Time Traps* (Nashville: Thomas Nelson, 2004).

Joseph L. Badaracco Jr., *Leading Quietly: An Unorthodox Guide to Doing the Right Thing* (Boston: Harvard Business School Press, 2002).

Stephen R. Covey, *First Things First* (New York: Simon & Schuster, 1994).

LESSON 12 LEADERSHIP COMMUNICATION

[F]ailure to listen increases cynicism and casts further doubt about leaders' intentions and trustworthiness. . . . Listening can't be achieved from a distance, by reading reports, or by hearing something secondhand. . . . Since proximity is the single best predictor of whether two people will talk to one another, we have to get close to people if we're going to communicate . . . we have to go to them.

—James M. Kouzes and Barry Z. Posner[34]

One of the most important tasks of a leader is communication; and for me, that task is one of the most difficult. Almost all of the failures I have had in leadership of my law firm over the past twelve years have been what Captain in the movie *Cool Hand Luke* would call a "failure to communicate." As more of an introverted person, I used to be quite content to sit alone in my office all day and bill hours for the financial benefit of my firm, rather than walking around to find out how the people I was supposed to be leading were doing. I am someone who is prone to communicate verbally in the most efficient manner possible. E-mail and quick, short directives therefore always seemed to be the most efficient and effective ways to communicate. However, I discovered that this communication style has hindered me in leading the firm effectively.

Face-to-face confrontation with others, especially other partners, can be quite difficult. Outsiders to the profession might assume that because law firm partners are lawyers they enjoy confronting each other. That has not been my experience. Holding the highest management position in my firm, I tended to address partner conduct issues indirectly. Early on when I discovered improper conduct by a fellow partner, I didn't confront it directly. Instead I brought the

---

34. *Credibility: How Leaders Gain and Lose It, Why People Demand It*, pages 99–100.

issue to my management committee and asked them to vote on a policy or procedure to address the breach. I would then issue an e-mail with the new policy or procedure, believing that a policy or procedure that applied uniformly would not single out the offender. What I found was initially quite baffling. Even though I had not singled them out by name, offenders would single themselves out with a scathing response for all to read, usually in defense of their prior conduct. After this occurred a few times, I realized that what I thought was an efficient and fair way to communicate was actually very divisive and ineffective. I needed to find a better and more effective way to communicate.

Leadership Thought and Application

Walk around and ask open-ended questions. You cannot know your followers' needs unless you communicate with them regularly and directly. This means getting out of your office—walking from workstation to workstation to talk to other members in the firm. If the firm has multiple offices, it also means regular visits to those offices. An organization's success depends on effective team leadership. You cannot lead if you are not actively pursuing a relationship with others in the organization. A leader who is a managing partner of a law firm tends to communicate mostly with other partners. In firms with a chief operating officer or firm administrator, administrative leaders usually handle communication with nonattorney staff, such as in the organization and conducting of staff meetings. Don't give in to the temptation to leave all nonattorney communication to administrators. Nonattorney professional staff need to believe that all of their firm leaders—not just administrative leaders—care about them. If staff know what is going on and what they can do to help, they are more likely to feel that they are integral to the organization and its success.

Henry Ford reportedly said, "Why is it that I always get the whole person, when what I really want is a pair of hands?" It's not one of his finer quotes. Leaders should want their people to think, to be a part of the organization, to believe they can make things better, and to actually make efforts to do so. All members of a law firm truly desire to be part of something more than just a job. It is the leader's task to tap into this desire.

E-mail and difficult feelings don't mix well. E-mail has clearly revolutionized society. In fact, it is difficult to remember what life was like before e-mail. An important difference between e-mail and face-to-face communication is what people are willing to say. For example, people who would rarely say thank you face-to-face may send e-mail messages of thanks. However, people seem more likely to share very difficult and potentially damaging emotions in e-mail, and that can hinder collaboration. For this reason, leaders need to implement, in their own use and among the firm, some basic e-mail guidelines.

A leader may receive an e-mail that evokes difficult emotions. Although the natural tendency is to immediately respond, consider the following alternatives:

1. **Try to delay your response.** If necessary, cool off. Then, if you respond, consider the best response from a leadership perspective.
2. **Choose whether to respond.** Every e-mail does not need a response. Sometimes the most appropriate response is no response at all. If the sender is trying to intimidate or display arrogance, it may be better not to reply by e-mail and instead address the issue in some other manner.
3. **Respond in person.** Although this alternative is not always available, within a firm a leader might use an in-person response as an opportunity to display leadership instead of sending an e-mail response in anger as an easy way out.

To remind yourself about appropriate internal communication, consider taping the following policy by an author unknown (found many years ago on the Internet) to the front of your computer, as a reminder.

"In general a positive tone is good—a negative, overly critical or unconstructive tone is not. The following are specific examples of undesirable behavior:

1. Needless, one- or two-word responses (such as *ditto, right on, yea* or *I agree*), or responses that are clearly directed toward one member, not the membership at large, and directed at another inappropriate e-mail by someone else.
2. Direct comments about other attorneys or staff that are abusive, derogatory or defamatory.
3. Comments that could be reasonably interpreted to be malicious in intent toward any other attorney or staff member.
4. An unnecessarily or intentionally negative or unconstructive tone in comments, opinions or suggestions about the firm, or any of its attorneys or staff.
5. Comments that are divisive with intent to segregate or polarize attorneys or staff.
6. Statements with blatant, malicious, unsubstantiated inaccurate or deceptive information.
7. Unsubstantiated comments, negative or positive, about staff or attorneys."

Practice active listening. Have you ever asked someone a question, started to listen to the answer, but then began to formulate a response before the other person finished speaking, perhaps even interrupting the person? If so, you are not alone. You are not really listening if you are thinking about a response before the other person finishes speaking. Listening is about much more than hearing words. It includes listening to tone and observing nonverbal signals. When you concentrate on your own thoughts, you miss these signals, and much of the verbal communication. By practicing active listening you can grasp the information and feelings being communicated. Active listening is about observing and trying to understand why another person feels the way he does, and what underlying message is truly being expressed and needs to be communicated.

Use nonaccusatory statements. This advice is typically given in premarriage counseling but is good advice for leaders in law firms. It is human nature to be lenient toward our own mistakes and cast blame on others when they may have erred. We understand our own motives, so we are lenient. In many cases our response to others is solely based on their actions. As a leader, instead of assuming motives and immediately casting blame when you see a mistake or error, take a deep breath, and ask questions. Instead of making accusatory statements, such as "You don't ever . . .," consider making statements about yourself and your response, along these lines: "It makes me feel . . . when . . ." Pay attention to the way you communicate with those you lead. If you concentrate on how the conduct of another makes you feel, others generally feel less threatened. Nonaccusatory communication shows that you are open-minded, want to understand, and have no interest in creating divisions within the firm.

Questions to Ponder

- Are you happy with your ability to communicate with others in your firm? If not, why not? If so, what are your weakest areas of communication and how can you improve them?
- Does your law firm have a problem with discourteous communication between members? If so, what strategies can be employed to train people to communicate more appropriately?

- Are you in the habit of listening to what you say—the words and the manner in which you say them—and asking yourself how it affects others?

Suggested Reading

James M. Kouzes and Barry Z. Posner, *Credibility: How Leaders Gain and Lose It, Why People Demand It* (San Francisco: Jossey Bass, 1993).

Steve Farber, *The Radical Leap: A Personal Lesson in Extreme Leadership* (Chicago: Dearborn Trade Publishing, 2004).

LESSON 13 ALONE TIME

> *Your thinking is the lid for your potential. If you're an excellent thinker, then you have excellent potential. . . . If people can keep growing in their thinking, they will constantly outgrow what they're doing.*
>
> —John C. Maxwell[35]

Earlier I mentioned how I was thrust into chairing the management committee of my firm and knew very little about management and leadership and the important roles they play in an individual's and firm's success. Once I learned the importance of leadership, I was determined to learn as much about it as I possibly could. It was not long before I realized that day-to-day management would generally crowd out any time I hoped to have for leadership education unless I took direct and intentional action to make it a priority. After reading *Thinking for a Change* by John Maxwell, I determined to set aside an hour each day to develop my personal leadership skills.

Considering that a day has twenty-four hours and up to a third of that time is devoted to sleep, an hour is a substantial block of time. Regardless, from what I had learned by then, setting aside one hour at least five days a week seemed more important in the long run. This hour was my Alone Time. At first I chose one hour at home when it was quiet, but I had a tendency to get up later in the morning, cutting my time short—sometimes to less than ten minutes before heading to the office. Then I made a commitment to arrive at work an hour earlier, when it was generally quiet. I did find, however, that I had to make sure the receptionist knew that this time was protected and would send all of my calls to voice mail. In addition, to be more effective, I did not open my e-mail until my Alone

---

35. *Thinking for a Change: 11 Ways Highly Successful People Approach Life and Work*, pages 11–12.

Time was over, and I turned off the e-mail notification, which is generally annoying and distracting.

Over the years, as my schedule, duties, and outside activities have changed, my Alone Time has varied, but it is still part of my routine because it has been a valuable tool in my development as a leader.

Leadership Thought and Application

Having a set time devoted to your own development and the future success of your firm is an important aspect of successful leadership. The amount of time and the specific principles and method of study will vary from leader to leader, though thirty minutes to an hour each day seems like a reasonable amount of time. Regardless, dedicating yourself to a regular daily undisturbed time for thought, contemplation, study, and planning will help you become a more successful leader. If you allow them to, today's immediate needs will always crowd out long-term growth activities. Leaders need to be disciplined enough to commit to, and keep, a regular daily time for education and growth. Consider these specific activities for Alone Time:

1. **Thinking.** In *Thinking for a Change*, Maxwell says that all highly successful leaders are good thinkers. In so many ways, people today seem to act before they think, instead of the other way around. Maxwell's book sets forth eleven thinking skills he believes that every leader should master. I believe that every lawyer leader needs to consider three of these skills as most important, regardless of whether he or she is leading a large or small firm or an entity or team of individuals within the firm.

    a. *Intentional thinking.* Day-to-day issues and worries can very easily sidetrack a busy lawyer so that he or she doesn't spend time thinking about strategy, planning, or potential problems. Thinking must be intentional and regular. You really do need to pick out a place for Alone

Time each day it is planned, and it needs to be protected from possible interruptions. You must also intentionally plan for balance in that time. You need time to think valuable thoughts and to allow thoughts to develop. Thinking does not mean deciding right away. Sometimes it will take quite a bit of time for an idea to develop into action. In fact, some thoughts that come to mind one day may never turn to action and, upon reflection might also seem like dumb ideas the next day.

b. *Big-picture thinking.* In most law firms, lawyers, including lawyer leaders, simply do not have time for long-range thinking. Clients have real problems or transactions to deal with every day, and they demand the time and attention of a trusted advisor. At the same time, law firms are business organizations with competitors from within and beyond the profession. Lawyer leaders need time to think more broadly about what the firm could do or be in the future. The type of thinking that a leader needs to do during Alone Time is not figuring out the details, but the big picture, perhaps considering new market segments, new ways to harness technology, new services that might be provided to existing clients, and so on. The big-picture thinker will envision the law firm as more than a traditional confederation of legal service providers who bill individual clients in increments of six minutes. The big-picture thinker will dream of a different type of law firm, one that is innovative and not only shaped to provide excellent client legal services but also organized in such a way to ultimately meet the expressed and unexpressed needs of clients.

c. *Strategic thinking.* With respect to a leader's personal development, strategic thinking must include time to strategize about the effective use of his or her own time.

In addition, a leader should think about major initiatives the firm has undertaken or may consider and examine the reasons behind them. Why are we considering this initiative? What are the real objectives? What resources are necessary, and how should the firm move forward? For instance, if the firm is thinking about opening an office in a smaller neighboring town, a leader might think about the issues related to that decision— what are the motivations to move forward, what needs to be done, what issues will the firm need to address, and how will they be handled? A leader does not need to make any decisions during this initial thinking during Alone Time. Thinking through these issues will help prepare the leader for discussion of the various considerations with the firm leadership group. Finally, a part of strategic thinking needs to also be dedicated to evaluating the firm's past and how successes can be replicated or challenges experienced, avoided.

2. **Study.** Spend a significant portion of your Alone Time in reading and study. This book is written so that it can be used as a tool during Alone Time. Each lesson includes reading, principles to apply, and questions to answer. Consider a variety of reading material, including textbooks, experiential texts, or leadership parables (such as those written by Patrick Lencioni or Andy Andrews), and biographies of famous or successful leaders. Consider books that describe U.S. presidents and international leaders (i.e., Churchill, Gordon Brown, Tony Blair, Ghandi, etc.). Include books about good and bad leaders, as you can learn lessons from both.

3. **Planning.** This kind of planning is not the strategic planning that every law firm needs. Instead it is about taking ideas that have been thought about and developed over several days and beginning to shape those thoughts intentionally

into potential actions. Some of this planning needs to be about the leader's own leadership skills and methods for handling day-to-day and strategic, long-range issues. Planning also needs to include some time regarding the firm as an organization, and a leader should document some of the action items that the full management team and ownership group should consider.

Questions to Ponder

- What would prevent you from committing to your own Alone Time every day? How can you remove these obstacles?
- What types of books do you read? Is your reading diverse? Is at least some of your reading regularly focused on leadership principles and training?
- When do you primarily focus on planning for your own future and that of your firm? Do day-to-day matters tend to crowd out planning for the future? What changes can you make in your everyday life to assure that you will have time to plan for the future?

Suggested Reading

John C. Maxwell, *Thinking for a Change: 11 Ways Highly Successful People Approach Life and Work* (New York: Time Warner Book Group, 2003).

Ken Blanchard and Phil Hodges, *Lead Like Jesus: Lessons from the Greatest Leadership Role Model of All Time* (Nashville: Thomas Nelson, 2005).

LESSON 14 TIME OFF

To manage the stress created by our leadership roles, we need personal time to relieve the tension.

—Bill George with Peter Sims[36]

The term *workaholic* is so commonly used that it is even in many dictionaries. Dictionary.Com defines *workaholic* as "a person who works compulsively at the expense of other pursuits," and *Collins English Dictionary* defines it as being "obsessively addicted to work." When I think of the stereotypical workaholic, I recall how television and movies portray this pattern of behavior and the devastating effects on the workaholics and those around them. In *The Family Man*, a movie from 2000, Nicolas Cage plays Jack Campbell, an aggressive, self-centered, and cutthroat investment banker. He has a very high position in the organization. Several people who work for him are trapped by his lifestyle and his expectations of them. The story is a modern version of *It's a Wonderful Life*. Campbell has everything, or so he thinks. Every hour of his life is focused on his work, and he even calls an emergency strategy meeting on Christmas morning, with plans to follow it by closing a business deal in the afternoon, and ending the day skiing alone in Colorado.

We really don't need to look at fictional movie portrayals to find workaholics. In many law firms I have observed, leaders at all levels generally do not have a life separate from work. Lawyers generally work long hours in the first place, but because leaders are expected to manage and lead while at the same time maintaining a robust book of business, workaholism seems to be the rule rather than the exception. I am familiar with a firm led by the same managing partner for more than twenty-five years. Only once in that time did the managing partner take a traditional vacation—one in which he left

---

36. *True North: Discover Your Authentic Leadership,* page 144.

town and did not come into the office for the duration. Some might say that managing partner was married to his job. When he finally stepped down, it was also time for him to retire. As with many marriages in which one spouse dies, the other dies soon afterward. Although this managing partner had planned to undertake many community initiatives during his retirement, his health began to decline within a year. And within four years of leaving this "marriage," this very effective leader passed away. His leadership and law practice were all he really had. Retirement seemed to accelerate the end of his life.

Lawyers, especially those who lead others, need a well-balanced life, one that includes a healthy dose of time off for rejuvenation and regeneration. But given the demands of leadership, is time off really possible, or is it just a pipe dream?

Leadership Thought and Application

Leading others is a tough job. Leadership speaker and author John Maxwell has said, "Leadership sucks." Of course, he says it in a way that gets a laugh, but he also says it to make a point: leadership is difficult and stressful, and it will definitely wear on a leader physically, emotionally, and mentally. Leadership of a law firm seems even more difficult and stressful because of the atypical organizational structure of most professional organizations. Consider these thoughts on taking time off:

1. **Define the leadership position but don't let it completely define you.** I am sure you have heard someone say, "I know I don't spend that much time with my kids, but the time I spend is quality time." That argument is usually made by people who don't identify strongly enough with their role as parent. There is no question that a leader will be, to a large extent, defined by his or her leadership position. At the same time, we each need to be defined by much more than just our

position or vocation; who we really are is defined by where we spend our time. Finding time for yourself—time away from the office—is first and foremost determined by your will. You must understand the importance of a well-rounded life and take intentional action to define your life holistically. If you don't control your identity but instead allow yourself to be defined by your work, you will not realize your dreams in life; in fact, you may forget them altogether. If you feel you have lost your multidimensional identity, challenge yourself to regain it. Start with your personal definition of success. How do you define it today? How did you define it the day before you assumed your current position? How will you define it on your deathbed? List the components you consider make a successful life. Be as comprehensive as possible. What have you achieved on that list? Have you lost sight of anything on it?

2. **Time off is not just for recuperation; it can also be for discovery of self and personal growth.** In some firms and organizations, leaders and managers understand the importance of time away from work beyond what is known as "vacation". These short breaks may be called sabbaticals, and leaders in larger organizations need to consider the benefits of one. Most organizations are not able to grant sabbaticals, so all leaders should view their time off—from a mental health day to a much longer vacation—as more than an opportunity to rest, recuperate, or get away. At least part of a leader's time away from the office should be devoted to reflection, discovery of self, and growth (one of the most important purposes of a sabbatical). Individuals have many options for devoting part of their time off to self-actualization. Some options are very expensive courses or retreats. At a minimum, leaders need to spend a portion of their time off

doing the same kinds of activities as during Alone Time (see Lesson 13).

3. **Stop wasting time, and you will have more time to take off.** Leadership is difficult in any organization. In a law firm it can be much more difficult. Firm owners elect or appoint one of their own members to fill a firm wide management position or to chair a substantive practice group. At the same time, the leader is generally expected to carry a full caseload. In many firms, the person selected is, and remains, one of the highest billers in the firm. That fact, in and of itself, makes it crucial for a leader to be a wise time manager. In many cases, the justification or excuse for not taking time off is that the leader is too busy; often, the real reason is poor time management. Many distractions in a law firm can cause lawyers to use time inefficiently. This inefficiency, in turn, can make lawyers too busy to take time off. Can you think of time-sapping activities in a law firm? Ask yourself if you are guilty of some of the following activities:

   a. **E-mail interruptions.** Interrupting billable work or management/leadership projects to respond to e-mails that can, and should, wait until later.

   b. **Too much socializing or wandering.** Obviously leaders need to spend some time walking around, creating relationships and communicating, but much of their work needs uninterrupted focus.

   c. **Nonbusiness use of the Internet.** Searching the Internet for non-work-related matters (political polls, sports scores, etc.) on work time.

   d. **Information overload.** Because so much leadership information is available (including books, blogs, and videos), it is easy to get bogged down by it. There is a fine line between not enough leadership education and too much.

e. **Failure to delegate.** Identify tasks that support staff and others can do and, as needed, teach them how to do the tasks. An upfront investment can pay off in the long term.

The true challenge for a leader is to balance total time available such that "I'm too busy" will no longer be an excuse for not taking time off or for having an imbalanced life.

4. **Total disengagement may be stressful.** Almost all law firm leaders are driven to accomplish. In some cases, total disengagement from work is both possible and necessary. In many instances, however, client and firm members expect leaders to be available 24-7, and total disengagement may be more stressful than minimal engagement while otherwise off the clock. If you will be stressed by not knowing what is going on at the office, consider limited—and disciplined—contact with the office. You might allocate ten to fifteen minutes each day to review e-mails and respond to true emergencies that cannot be delegated. Resist the temptation to expand the definition of a true emergency by limiting the time you spend on firm business. You may find that this very limited contact reduces your stress during the last few days of your time off because you will be less concerned about what is waiting for you when you return.

Questions to Ponder

- Is your identity, or what defines you, completely tied or related to your leadership position or your work?
- What compels you to give more and more of your time to your leadership position? What can be done to help you live a more balanced life, where you can remain committed to the

organization and also have a reasonable life apart from your position?

- Has an unbalanced identity interfered with your ability to realize your dreams? Do you have any dreams to realize outside of your leadership position or work?

Suggested Reading

John Izzo, *Second Innocence: Rediscovering Joy and Wonder* (San Francisco: Barrett-Koehler 2004).

Bill Gates Sr., *Showing Up for Life: Thoughts on the Gift of a Lifetime* (New York: Random House 2009).

LESSON 15 STRENGTHS VS. WEAKNESSES

Concentrate on your strengths. . . . Waste as little effort as possible on improving areas of low competence.

—Peter F. Drucker[37]

After graduation from Wake Forest University School of Law and a short employment with a large Winston-Salem law firm, I took a position as an associate with a solo practitioner in a small town in western North Carolina. Because my wife and I were raised in a much larger suburban area near Washington, DC, and though there were a few things we did like about small town life, there was much about it that we did not enjoy. My employer was a true general practitioner. Though I learned the pitfalls of trying to be a jack-of-all-trades, master of none, I also gained a wide experience in the practice of law. I learned valuable lessons about my strengths and weaknesses as I tried my hand in real property transactions and disputes, commercial transactions and litigation, preparation of wills, and estate controversies. My employer also required me to handle court-appointed criminal matters. This broad experience allowed me to discover that my gifts in the practice of law are in transactional settings and not areas involving controversy or litigation. I realized that I express myself much better in writing than through public speaking. I was so uncomfortable with the oral part of litigation that my nervousness caused physical ailments. These two years gave me great insight into my strengths and weaknesses.

Every law firm leader must discover his or her strengths and weaknesses. This learning process is time-consuming and crucial to the success of the organization. Early on in my leadership development, I took the well-known Myers-Briggs personality test and found that I am more of an introvert and generally less of a

---

37. *The Essential Drucker*, pages 218–220.

touchy-feely type of person. For the other management and administrative positions in my firm, the firm owners have generally elected people with strengths that complement my weaknesses. At times, our management team did not have complementary strengths and weaknesses, and I believe the firm suffered for it.

Two examples from my twelve years of law firm leadership illustrate the need for complementary strengths and weaknesses. The first example is our firm president, a senior partner and a former mayor of Asheville. One of my areas of weakness in the early years was building consensus, compounded by the fact that I was one of the youngest partners in the firm. Building consensus or gaining buy-in comes as a natural way of life for the firm president. He has had many years of practice, within the law firm and local and state politics. The second example is the firm's most recent chief operating officer, who is also a certified public accountant. Unlike many numbers people, this COO is an extrovert, who connected with our staff quite well. While he was with our firm, his greatest value to me was that we were a team with complementary strengths and weaknesses. As an introvert I tend to focus on a project and not come up for air until it is completed. Because of his complementary strengths, we were able to get much work done and also build relationships, trust, and a sense of security among those we led.

Leadership Thought and Application

Although most people think they have identified their strengths and weaknesses, their conclusions are generally uneducated guesses. It is critical that every lawyer leader understand his or her true strengths and weaknesses, and those of every member of the leadership team. Consider the following basic truths about leadership strengths and weaknesses:

Be aware of personal strengths and weaknesses. A leader should not assume what his or her strengths and weaknesses are. To truly identify these, a leader might get help from a mentor or coach (see Lesson 9), especially one who has observed the leader in action. On his or her own, a leader may use personal questions to identify strengths and weaknesses, perhaps during Alone Time (see Lesson 13). To discover strengths, ask: At what points in my activities, action, or leadership do I feel most empowered, successful, or fulfilled? To discover weaknesses, ask: At what points in my activities, actions, or leadership do I feel scared, apprehensive, in despair, intimidated, or physically drained?

Build up your strengths. Discovering your strengths and weaknesses is not rocket science. Various personality and leadership tests can give you an idea about them. Myers-Briggs is probably the most famous personality test, and it also reveals important information about an individual's leadership skills. In the realm of leadership, *Leadership 2.0* by Travis Bradberry and Jean Greaves[38] comes with 360° Refined, a free online leadership skills test; John Maxwell has developed another skills test, the 360° Leader Comprehensive Assessment (see www.johnmaxwell.com). Though there are many such tools available, the best way to identify strengths and weaknesses is introspection and honest feedback from people whom you trust and who have seen you in action. Once you have an idea of your leadership strengths and weaknesses, avoid a traditional grade-school approach to leadership development. The same curriculum will not work for everyone, and trying to remediate weaknesses is usually a waste of time. Almost all leadership experts have concluded that leaders should spend their time developing strengths and not weaknesses. For example, on a scale of one to ten (ten being the highest level of skill), if you are an eight in one area and a three in another, spend your time working to change the eight to a nine or ten, which might make you world-class in that area. No matter how hard you

---

38. Travis Bradberry and Jean Greaves, *Leadership 2.0* (San Diego: TalentSmart, 2012).

work to change the three, you might achieve a modest increase to four or five, which is still objectively a failure.

Surround yourself with a team. Leaders need trusted advisors who have strengths in their areas of weakness. In a law firm this means a diverse management committee or governing board that includes members who complement each other. Members of leadership teams such as executive committees, who have common goals and objectives, should feel at ease discussing with each other their individual strengths and weaknesses, and assign tasks and duties accordingly.

Questions to Ponder

- Are you certain that you have identified your strengths and weaknesses? How have you confirmed your beliefs?
- Do you focus more on developing your strengths or your weaknesses?
- Can you identify your colleagues' strengths and weaknesses? Do you rely on others' strengths, or do you feel inadequate when you know others are strong in your areas of weakness?

Suggested Reading

Peter F. Drucker, *The Essential Drucker* (New York: Harper-Collins, 2001).

Marcus Buckingham, *The Truth about You: Your Secret to Success* (Nashville: Thomas Nelson, 2008).

Discipline 3

Success

Success is peace of mind which is a direct result of self-satisfaction in knowing you made the effort to become the best of which you are capable.

—John Wooden and Steve Jamison[39]

Years ago, before we used electronic devices for reading, two books were in every Hilton Hotel guest room: the Holy Bible and *Be My Guest* by Conrad Hilton.[40] *Be My Guest* is mostly an autobiography describing Hilton's early years of poverty and his actions during the Depression that made him a millionaire. This paperback book certainly offers many leadership lessons. However, the book concludes with a nonbiographical chapter about leadership titled "There Is an Art to Living." The chapter begins as follows:

> Each of us strives for success. The housewife, the statesman, the carpenter, saint or businessman, for each forward momentum is established by the desire to accomplish, prosper, grow in his chosen field. What is this thing—success? It cannot be measured by the accumulation of money. Too many rich men are failures and too many poor men masters at the art of living to make this the criterion. . . . The yardstick for measuring success would seem to be not how much a man gets as how much he has to give away. . . . The true fruits of successful living are not

---

39. *Wooden* (New York: McGraw-Hill, 2005), page 3.
40. Conrad Hilton, *Be My Guest* (New York: Prentice Hall, 1957).

material. They are contentment, the joy or usefulness, growth through the fulfillment of a particular talent.

Hilton then goes on to set out and explain the ten ingredients that must be blended to live successfully:

1. Find your own particular talent.
2. Be big: Think big. Act big. Dream big.
3. Be honest.
4. Live with enthusiasm.
5. Don't let your possessions possess you.
6. Don't worry about your problems.
7. Don't cling to the past.
8. Look up to people when you can—down to no one.
9. Assume your full share of responsibility for the world in which you live.
10. Pray constantly and confidently.[41]

For every leader, these are valuable principles to live by. In addition, every law firm leader needs to understand a few additional guidelines that will lead to success:

- First, every leader needs to understand that failure is not the opposite of success, and it usually presents unique and valuable opportunities for learning and growth.
- Second, much can be learned from prior leaders of the firm, and the success of the firm will, in many ways, be determined by how followers view the treatment of those prior leaders.
- Third, it is important for every leader to be driven in leadership by a true desire to see others (those who follow) succeed. This is a very basic role of every servant leader.

---
41. Hilton, pages 279–288.

LESSON 16 FAILURE IS NOT THE OPPOSITE OF SUCCESS

A leader must recognize that, in the end, there are worse things than even defeat. When facts dictate that one's business has failed, or that one's war is lost, and that no further effort could possibly achieve success, a leader knows it is far better to face facts squarely than to carry on a struggle that results only in needless effusions of red ink.

—H. W. Crocker III[42]

Do you agree with the title of this chapter, that failure is not the opposite of success? If you do, you are not alone. In fact, what happens after failure or success is many times more important than the initial result of either. Failures and successes are true opportunities for leaders. The danger with success, especially ongoing success, is complacency. Failure may cause concern that the organization will spiral downward into many more failures. In most cases, however, a failure is an opportunity for leadership growth. Failure provides a way to learn from your mistakes so you don't make them again and can use the experience to move forward.

Leadership failures come in many forms. One extreme example is the failure of a prominent law firm leader and father of a judge. A news article reported that the lawyer had convinced clients, including some who had known him for years and trusted him completely, to invest in a type of Ponzi scheme. Certainly this leadership failure is not likely to lead to redemption or restoration to his leadership position, regardless of whether the leader learns lessons and makes changes in his life.

---

42. *Robert E. Lee on Leadership: Executive Lessons in Character, Courage, and Vision*, page 161.

A more typical leadership failure involves a failure in judgment or execution; for instance, a decision to push the firm into a new practice area when a little study would have revealed that the business model would not support the commitment. Another example is a law firm leader who is overwhelmed by the personality and interview skill (and representations) of a young lawyer job applicant, only to find out that a little due diligence would have revealed that the individual is not a good fit for the collaborative culture of the firm.

An example from my own firm is a decision we made about eight years ago to jump into a personal injury marketing campaign without adequate research into what might work in our unique community. Without adequate planning and preparation, we ended up with advertisements and expensive yellow pages listings, but no thriving practice to show for it. It was a simple failure with short-term financial loss and fortunately no long-term consequences. Some might argue that we did not give the campaign enough time, but considering the way prospective clients now procure legal services, and the effectiveness of certain types of marketing, I firmly believe it was a mistake that gave us an opportunity to learn about effective marketing.

Leadership Thought and Application

Fearing failure is certainly no way for a leader to live life. For many very successful businesspeople, the path to success began through failure. Constant fear of failure can cause a leader to miss out on opportunities for success. Leaders who desire long-term success need to recognize that the path is long and that the rapid pace of change may make today's failures tomorrow's successes.

Getting to success may mean a long hard journey. For a new leader who is afraid of failure, the path may be long and hard. A law firm leader chosen by his or her peers (regardless of the position) truly desires to do a good job. Constant fear does not lead to success, and it's no way to live. Every person in a position of leadership will inevitably make a bad decision and fail in his or her own eyes or those of others. Simply recognizing this fact early on makes eventual success more likely. The key is to have a plan of response to failure:

1. **Own up to it.** Lawyers, most of whom are proud by nature, may have difficulty believing they could make a mistake, much less fail. Don't try to sugar-coat failure or hide or disguise it from your firm. Own up to it and take responsibility for it. Followers will respect you all the more and will appreciate that you kept them involved. Owning the failure provides a perfect opportunity to obtain feedback, and others may have a different perspective about the process or outcome.

2. **Learn from it.** Most people want to avoid mistakes, and they certainly do not want to repeat them. Understanding and learning from mistakes is the best insurance against repeat performances. But people who know that even skilled leaders experience failures are usually more willing to learn from their own mistakes. They can use the counsel and advice of trusted peers and the insight of a mentor or coach to help analyze their mistakes. In addition, a mentor or coach may be able to share personal experience. Another good way to learn from mistakes is by comparing your actions with those of other leaders, including leaders outside the legal profession. How did they handle failure? Whom did they blame? How did they handle similar situations when confronted a second or third time?

3. **Have a plan to not repeat it.** In many cases, a mistake or failure can be traced to specific precursors; for example, certain policies and procedures or strategies and goals that the leader has established. If a leader is able to identify the precursors, he or she can create and implement a comprehensive plan so that the same mistake will not recur. Instead of

reacting (or overreacting) emotionally if a similar issue or circumstance arises again, a leader can review the plan. Of course, in many cases, action is needed before a written plan can be reviewed, but initially developing the plan prepares the leader to respond calmly and rationally, so that another mistake can usually be avoided.

The rapid pace of change. A decision that results in a mistake or failure may simply be bad timing. Leaders tend to be forward thinking and often want to make changes before the other members of their organization are ready to follow. As a result, support for the change is lacking, so it becomes a failure or mistake. In law firms, which are notoriously conservative about taking risks or making changes, this effect may be more pronounced. Leaders need to consider whether the failure is a result of timing and, if so, try again at a better time. So in some cases, the adage *"If at first you don't succeed, try, try, again"* applies.

Questions to Ponder

- Can you think of a time that you failed in your leadership at your firm? How did followers react? How did you react? Did you take responsibility for the failure or mistake? Did you deflect blame?
- Are there worse things than defeat or failure for a leader? What are they? What causes something to be worse than defeat or failure?
- Are you more enthusiastic about change in the firm than are your peers? Have you ever experienced failure because an activity or action was simply ahead of its time for your firm? If so, what was that activity or action? Did failure make you less likely to want to try again?

Suggested Reading

H. W. Crocker III, *Robert E. Lee on Leadership: Executive Lessons in Character, Courage, and Vision* (Roseville, CA: Prima Publishing, 1999).

Brian D. Biro, *Beyond Success: The 15 Secrets to Effective Leadership and Life Based on Legendary Coach John Wooden's Pyramid of Success* (New York: Penguin Putnam 1997).

LESSON 17 LEARN FROM THE PAST—
HONOR AND RESPECT PROVEN LEADERS

> *All leaders are influenced by those they admire. Reading about them and studying their development inevitably allows an aspiring leader to grow his own leadership traits. If he's lucky, he'll be able to learn from leaders in his own life—ask them questions, observe them in private, determine which of that leader's methods work well and would complement his own burgeoning style.*
>
> —Rudolph W. Guiliani[43]

> *Leaders take lessons from the past, but never sacrifice the future for the sake of mere continuity. People of vision gauge decisions on the future; the story of the past cannot be rewritten.*
>
> —J. Oswald Sanders[44]

I have observed a common leadership problem in many law firms. When a leader steps down, members are publicly respectful but do not truly respect the former leader. This lack of respect can be a result of the new leader failing to understand the feelings and commitment of former leaders. My observation is that as members rise to leadership positions, they are so busy that they do not have time to understand and recognize the commitment of those former leaders. Whether the new leader agrees with the decisions and directions of past leadership, and notwithstanding whether the firm will embark on a new direction, new leaders need to recognize that former leaders have sacrificed personally and professionally. (To

---

43. *Leadership*, page xiv.
44. *Spiritual Leadership*, Chapter 8, n.p.

appreciate this potential lack of respect, consider the future when your successor reflects on your leadership tenure.)

Unfortunately, honor and respect for past leadership are not the norm in business or politics. Obviously in politics, huge egos are involved, and the rise of negative campaigning results in the commonplace campaign tool of dishonoring the current office-holder (even if that person is not running for reelection). In business we see more of the same, just without commercials. Compounding the problem is the fact that many leaders of corporations depart in disgrace, or with shamefully large golden parachutes.

There are some bright spots, however, including within the legal profession. The late Ed Flitton, a good friend until his untimely death in 2010, was a former managing partner of the four-hundred–member firm of Holland & Hart, the largest law firm based in the Mountain West. Ed was one of the few people I counted among my law firm leadership coaches. He stepped down from his management position shortly after I got to know him quite well. He and I spent many hours at ABA meetings talking about law firm leadership. Ed loved his firm and often expressed how much he enjoyed leading it. He continued to be associated with his law firm after stepping down and enjoyed his continued association with it, calling it his professional home. I have no doubt that a major part of his continuing satisfaction was due to the honor and respect he was shown over the years and after his retirement. This was expressed on the Holland & Hart post after Ed passed away, when the firm chairman, John Husband, stated, "Ed was the gold standard as a leader, lawyer and friend. He was thoughtful, respectful, reasoned and considerate in his views and advice."

Leadership Thought and Application

The leader of an organization needs to understand and respect the efforts and accomplishments of those who have gone before. At times, however, this is easier said than done.

Honor and respect. No matter the circumstance, you should consider honor and respect of former leaders as a priority. Circumstances will dictate how to acknowledge the former leader. If the departure was difficult, it might be challenging. Assuming that a former leader will still be a member of your firm (whether in an of-counsel position or retired but present), you need a plan to incorporate him or her into firm functions. Consider whether your inactive former leaders will still have office space within your facility. If the former leader will still be an active partner, participation will already be invited and encouraged. In any event, how you communicate to others in the firm or to the public should be positive and respectful of the former leader's sacrifices. It is crucial to understand that the other members in the law firm will be watching to see how you act toward your former leaders. It will say much about you and how you will treat others.

Useful engagement. Prior leaders who remain with your firm need to be actively engaged. Often a former leader is a potential coach for a new leader. If this is not appropriate, perhaps the outgoing leader can mentor or coach an associate or be a special advisor to a practice group. Even if a former leader steps down under difficult circumstances, some significant position of honor or respect might go a long way to mend a damaged relationship.

Support in practice. In many cases, a former leader will need to reestablish a practice that has been substantially depleted because of the time commitments of management and leadership. New firm leaders can show respect with patience and support of a past leader while he or she reestablishes a full caseload.

Communication. New leaders will often desire to make changes; this desire is common and expected. In addition, former leaders generally are proud of their accomplishments. Because a key objective of current leadership should be to keep past leaders involved and happy, consider giving former leaders advance notice of significant changes (especially if the change affects an initiative that the prior leader owns or is proud of.) At the same time, express thanks for past accomplishments in the areas where change is being considered or made. It is important that past leaders do not feel betrayed. The last thing you want is for a potentially productive and helpful former leader and partner to leave and become a productive member of (or of counsel to) a competitive firm down the street.

Questions to Ponder

- Do you feel that you honor and respect past leaders of your firm? How do you show your respect? In what ways can you do a better job in honoring them?
- What are some unique ways that you have involved retired leaders of your firm? Do retired members have office space and other resources at your business location?
- Does your firm have a fair plan to allow former leaders to reengage in practice after they have stepped down from leadership?

Suggested Reading

Patrick J. McKenna and Brian Burke, *Serving at the Pleasure of My Partners: Advice to the New Firm Leader* (Danvers, MA: Thomson Reuters, 2011).

Richard Brookhiser, *George Washington on Leadership* (Philadelphia: Basic Books, 2008).

J. Oswald Sanders, *Spiritual Leadership* (Chicago: Moody Publishers, 1967).

Mark Sanborn, *The Encore Effect* (New York: Random House 2008).

LESSON 18 BE DRIVEN BY THE DESIRE TO SEE OTHERS SUCCEED

Albert Einstein said it best: "Only a life lived in the service to others is worth living." . . . Contrary to conventional wisdom, the bottom line of a career is not how far you advance yourself, but how far you advanced and served others.

—John C. Maxwell, Stephen R. Graves, and Thomas G. Addington[45]

Pride, arrogance, and self-centeredness are often characteristics attributed to leaders. Members of an organization may perceive their leaders as only looking out for themselves, wanting fame or glory, taking credit for the success of others, or desiring to be seen as great. This image is perpetuated in our society, especially in the media. For example, the movie *Wall Street* portrays Gordon Gecko, a greedy business leader. In real life the news media commonly suspect that business owners have gained wealth at the expense of others.

The media also frequently portrays lawyers as greedy. Television shows and movies frequently perpetuate this stereotype about lawyers and the legal profession. The movie *The Firm* and the character Jackie Chiles on television's *Seinfeld* come to mind. The facts may be different, but some of the foolish pseudo-marketing activities lawyers put on the Internet have also perpetuated the stereotype.

Notwithstanding this stereotype, many law firm leaders are true leaders because they have made their own interests subservient to the firm and truly desire to see others in the organization succeed. My friend Linda Klein is such a leader. She is the managing partner of the Atlanta office of Baker Donelson, a firm based in Memphis, Tennessee. Linda's extraordinary leadership talents benefit her firm, community, state and local bar associations, and the American Bar

---
45. *Life@Work: Marketplace Success for People of Faith,* pages 148–149.

Association. She exemplifies a Level 5 leader, according to Jim Collins. He says that leaders like Linda

> channel their ego away from themselves and into a larger goal of building a great company. It's not that Level 5 leaders have no ego or self-interest. Indeed, they are incredibly ambitious; but their ambition is first and foremost for the institution, not themselves. . . . Level 5 leaders are a study in duality: modest and willful, humble and fearless.[46]

Collins goes on to describe one Level 5 leader he knows as "making anything he touched the best it could possibly be."[47] This description fits Linda; what she touches are the lives of those who work with her and her law firm. Over the past few years, she has described to me the ways she has used firm strategies, policies, and procedures to further her firm's mission and vision. Every initiative she has shared with me makes the members of her firm who are involved look better by actually being better; they are better for their clients, better for their colleagues, and better for the firm.

Leadership Thought and Application

Although in good faith and with the best intentions for the organization, a law firm leader might adopt an erroneous but common definition of personal success that is tied to results. For example, a leader might feel successful if the firm achieves some positive result, perhaps based on an objective performance measure such as profits per partner. Instead, success is properly viewed as employing a more valid or useful process, the result of which is positive. In other words, a leader's true success is tied to the success of those in the organization.

A leader's priority should always be the desire to enable others in the firm to succeed. A natural consequence of others' success is the

---
46. Jim Collins, *Good to Great* (New York: Harper-Collins, 2001), pages 21–22.
47. Ibid., 23.

leader's success. Consider these principles, attitudes, and actions as you strive to enable others' success:

An altruistic desire. The concern to see others succeed should be genuine; otherwise followers will see through the facade. An altruistic desire is displayed through an unselfish concern and devotion to those being led. This desire is exhibited in a number of ways:

- patience with others as they attempt to achieve goals and objectives
- encouragement and enthusiasm for the efforts and work of those being led
- trust in followers and the work they are pursuing, without micromanagement
- an attitude which is not self-serving, but puts others' needs before the leader's

A generous heart. Leaders must make organizational decisions to benefit followers. Such decisions mean followers will be more likely to succeed in carrying out their part of the firm's mission. Leaders also need to do their best to provide appropriate resources so firm members can achieve their goals. In fact, leaders should seek out ways to support their followers and help assure their success.

Empowerment of others. A leader should establish less controlling and more empowering policies and procedures. Such policies and procedures allow members of the firm to be themselves professionally and personally, which contributes to their success. However, a firm leader should not have a laissez-faire attitude. As previously stated, appropriate influence is not about the power of position; instead it is persuasion—a gentle, willful, and persistent influence. It is about an effort to move those led to succeed.

Questions to Ponder

- Think of a few positive (selfless) and negative (selfish) examples of leaders. What do you think was the biggest difference between the attitude and focus of these two types of leaders? As a leader, what is your definition of success? Is it tied to your own achievement, the firm's achievement, or individual members' achievement?
- Do you have an altruistic desire to see others succeed? How patient are you with others when they fail? If your patience is lacking, why is that the case?
- What steps in your quest to see others succeed can you take to empower followers within the firm? Do you have enough trust to let go and empower others? How can you both empower and appropriately oversee and encourage?

Suggested Reading

John C. Maxwell, Stephen R. Graves, and Thomas G. Addington, *Life@Work: Marketplace Success for People of Faith* (Nashville: Thomas Nelson, Inc., 2005).

Andrew Elowitt, *The Lawyer's Guide to Professional Coaching* (Chicago: American Bar Association, 2012).

Discipline 4
Fulfillment

[A] dream is an inspiring picture of the future that energizes your mind, will, and emotions, empowering you to do everything you can to achieve it. A dream worth pursuing is a picture and blueprint of a person's purpose and potential.

—John C. Maxwell[48]

True fulfillment is elusive to most of us. Some people, even those in the highest management and leadership positions, simply do not like what they do day-to-day. They may be highly paid, but they do not experience joy and satisfaction, in spite of the outward success they seem to have. For others, the opposite is true. In fact, some leaders appear to find so much satisfaction in their position that they would consider doing it without compensation. What causes this difference? How do the leaders who truly enjoy their positions manage the ongoing stress of leading others without cracking under the pressure?

In his book *Second Innocence: Rediscovering Joy and Wonder*, John Izzo describes finding joy in your work and leadership position:

> Our jobs are almost always bigger than we are. And one of the keys to staying in love with our work is to continue to see the wonder available to us at work, to always see the noble possibilities in our role. One manager sees his job as making the payroll; another sees herself as mentoring young people. . . . [A] large part of leadership is to help others see the

---

48. *Put Your Dream to the Test: Ten Questions to Help You See It and Seize It* (Nashville: Thomas Nelson, 2009), page xiii.

deeper possibilities in their roles. . . . How do we fall in love with our work? I think we must never forget that we are always on holy ground if our eyes are open. We must never stop looking with innocent wonder at what our jobs might produce if we bring more of ourselves to them. . . . Is it possible that whatever you are doing, your true work is nobler than you think? When we see the possibilities in each moment, when we reflect on how we can save the world a little bit in every interaction we have and in every role we play, life changes in wonderful and mysterious ways.[49]

Izzo suggests a mind-set that can turn any position into one of fulfillment. The three lessons to follow in this section are all about fulfillment. First, no matter how much time you spend being successful as a leader, and no matter how successful you appear to be, you will not be truly fulfilled in your position unless you enjoy it. Leadership, even for a leader in a law firm filled with numerous autonomous lawyers, should be fun. Not everyone is meant for a position of leadership or management in a law firm. If you are not having fun in your position, maybe the position is not right for you, or perhaps you should change your outlook on life. Second, leaders are unique individuals, but the basic leadership laws apply to all of them: Each leader has different strengths and weaknesses and different ways of getting things done. A leader who discovers his or her authentic voice—the leader's core beliefs and values—can find true fulfillment in leadership. The authentic voice of a leader comes from discovering that leadership is not just a job but a calling, one that is expressed uniquely in accordance with the leader's values and beliefs. These values and beliefs should be consistent with the values and beliefs of others in the law firm. Finally, part of a leader's fulfillment comes from the safety and power followers find in the leader's presence.

---

49. John Izzo, *Second Innocence: Rediscovering Joy and Wonder* (San Francisco: Berrett-Koehler, 2004), pages 70–72.

LESSON 19 LEADERSHIP SHOULD BE FUN

The servant leader models having fun and promotes having fun. . . . Spirited leaders have fun giving and sharing credit. They believe fun is nourishment for the soul. . . . Fun and joy are not luxuries, they are necessary for spirit to grow.

—Ellen Castro[50]

How do you define *fun*? Is it the way you normally describe your life in the practice of law? Does it accurately describe your role as a leader? In his book *Joy at Work*, Dennis Bakke indicates that members of his organization, during a process of strategic planning, defined *fun* as "rewarding, exciting, creative, and successful."[51] Given this definition, leadership of a law firm can be fun for someone with the right attitude, purpose, and goals for the firm and his or her role in it.

Many people who practice law might say that they feel this way about their legal work or specific clients they represent and interact with. In my experience, however, most law firm leaders would not describe their role as fun, and rarely would a managing partner describe a partner meeting as fun.

A practice group leader of a firm shared with me that he was scared of a member of his practice group, and he was serious. He dreaded scheduling meetings of the practice group because he simply did not want to deal with this member. His fright was not a result of anything physically threatening; he simply did not like confrontation. A managing partner of another firm told me that partner meetings had become "a mental, emotional, and physical drain" and that he had aged more than ten years in the mere two years he had actually been in the role. Clearly, these lawyer leaders were not having a whole lot of fun.

---

50. *Spirited Leadership: 52 Ways to Build Trust on the Job,* page 124.
51. *Joy at Work*, page 24.

On the other hand, the Summit Law Group in Seattle, Washington, has as one of its written core values "To have fun" (see www.summitlaw.com). Can fun really be a core value in a for-profit law firm? Or is that just a platitude without substance? And if it is a core value for the firm, how does it relate to the concept of fun for a leader?

Firms in which leaders have negative attitudes about their leadership role (including the two firms previously mentioned) seem to have common characteristics. To one extent or another, they lack shared values, authority, and achievement. In the Summit Law Group, however, it seems that this kind of organizational sharing may be the norm. This firm has a stated set of core values shared by all lawyers and staff, and it has broken down hierarchies that are quite typical in law firms, by replacing common power systems with measures of empowerment and getting rid of the barriers created by such simple things as office location and decoration.

Leadership Thought and Application

Shared values. Part of a good strategic planning process for any law firm must include determining the values that the organization recognizes as important to its success (*success* being defined broadly). In many firms the planning process may not include associate or staff members. Including these people in the process can have benefits, especially increased acceptance of firm values. Failure to include everyone in the firm is not fatal to getting this values buy-in, but understand that without a buy-in to shared values among members, the role of the leader is anything but fun.

Without shared values some members of the firm could easily see their positions as just jobs. They may not be invested in the firm's future or may feel that they are mindlessly following orders. Leadership will be more exciting when each firm member understands where the firm is headed, why it is headed that way, and collectively where the members will be when they get there. It should be the desire of every law firm leader to see the firm as his or her mission. An important goal for every leader is to help everyone employed by the firm—not just owners—to see the mission in the same way. Consider the following ideas to encourage shared values in the firm:

1. Involve representatives of as many different practice groups, departments, and firm levels (staff, associates, partners, members with different offices) as possible in developing a strategic planning process. Involve everyone in the organization, to one extent or another, some involvement in considering and determining the firm's shared values.

2. In staff meetings and meetings of firm lawyers, discuss the firm's shared values. Allow time for others to offer input and suggestions, ask questions, and voice concerns about how the firm can live up to its values and still achieve its mission. Conduct regular meetings and include some form of mutual accountability.

3. Make sure that the members of any practice groups, departments, or committees see the goals of these entities in the context of the organization's shared values.

Shared authority. Many leadership speakers use the Ritz-Carlton Corporation as an example of a company that has excelled in the area of shared authority through its Employee Empowerment Plan. (The program is so noteworthy that Ritz-Carlton leaders believe that the term *empowerment* originated with their company.) In this program, Ritz-Carlton gives each employee the discretion to spend up to $2,000 of the hotel's funds to solve a guest's problem immediately, without checking with a supervisor. This program has two important results. Employees are much less likely to neglect difficult situations with the excuse that it's not their job. In addition, the program makes employees feel they are a valuable and important part of the company. Decision-making power in the area of customer service gives employees an authentic sense of shared authority. Within limits, employees can step outside of their job description without worrying about whether their decisions will be questioned.

The system that Ritz-Carlton uses, at least to the tune of $2,000 per employee, might not be economically feasible for a law firm. However, a lack of authority sharing in a law firm most often leads to feelings of dissatisfaction, oppression, and helplessness. None of these feelings are conducive to a fun workplace. Shared authority, however, can lead to a feeling of excitement and foster creativity, among firm members. Having creative and excited followers will certainly make the position of the leader more enjoyable. Consider the following possible ways to share authority in the firm:

1. Find significant roles for representatives from staff, associates, and partners to participate in decision making about future direction, serve on organization committees, and educate others about practice management tools and practices.
2. To the extent permitted by the Rules of Professional Conduct, give nonpartners some authority in decision making, such as the ability to make or authorize limited purchases related to their work performance.
3. Give followers regular opportunities to perform functions other than the routine client work of "minding" or "grinding." Allow members some time to research innovative ways to do their work as well as new areas of service they might perform for firm clients.

Shared achievement. From the smallest mom-and-pop business or solo law firm to the United States government or the largest multinational law practice, most of the blame and accolades generally go to the leaders. While it may not be fair for a leader to take the full blame for a situation, it is really his or her job to sacrifice for those being led, even if it means taking the first cut in pay or whatever other pain may come in times of trouble. If the firm leader accepts most of the praise for something that the organization—or even the leader—has accomplished, it can be harmful to the idea of having fun at work, even for the leader.

Leadership will only be fun for a leader if it is rewarding for followers. If followers believe that the leader is taking all of the credit and other rewards for success, the followers will be individually and collectively disappointed. Dealing with the resulting negativity will certainly not be fun, and it will dampen any sense of achievement, success, or fulfillment for the leader. But sharing the benefits of personal and organizational success leads to a positive—and fun—climate (good karma). Leaders might consider these ideas:

1. When a firm lawyer receives any kind of public recognition (for example, an acknowledgment of local charitable work, national award from a professional association, etc.), the leader needs to publicize the achievement within the firm, specifically recognizing those who have contributed to the individual's success.

2. In successful practice-related accomplishments, such as a positive result in a litigation matter, a leader should make a point to recognize junior members of the firm (including support staff) who were involved.

3. The leader should attend staff meetings and recognize, specifically, the efforts and achievements of staff.

4. In law firms with distinct practice groups, there may be a tendency to recognize only the litigators' achievements in the courtroom or success in settlement. However, leaders need to make a point of recognizing the achievements of other members of the firm, especially transactional lawyers who might not have such well-defined success points. A leader can recognize such success points during a meeting by asking someone

what he or she is working on. This kind of recognition is even more effective when a leader finds out this information beforehand and shares it himself or herself.

5. All of the above are means of public recognition. In many firms everyone in the firm receives an e-mail announcing congratulations for a success. Members often send me-too e-mails adding their congratulations. However, one of the most meaningful acknowledgments is a private acknowledgment from the leader who goes to a staff member, associate, or partner and verbally expresses his or her appreciation for, and recognition of, the achievement.

Questions to Ponder

- Would you describe your position of leadership as fun? If not, why not?
- Do you agree that shared values among firm members will lead to greater creativity? As a leader, do you encourage creativity from members of the firm? What are the ways that you can foster greater creativity in your organization?
- To what extent have you shared some of the authority for decision making with others in your law firm? What other ways can you empower your members?

Suggested Reading

Ellen Castro, *Spirited Leadership: 52 Ways to Build Trust on the Job* (Notre Dame, IN: Ave Maria Press, 1998).

Dennis W. Bakke, *Joy at Work: A Revolutionary Approach to Fun on the Job* (Seattle: PVG, 2005).

LESSON 20 FINDING YOUR AUTHENTIC VOICE

Voice is unique personal significance—significance that is revealed as we face our greatest challenges and which makes us equal to them. . . . When you engage in work that taps your talent and fuels your passion . . . therein lies your voice, your calling, your soul's code.

—Stephen R. Covey[52]

There is an inspirational movie I watch almost every time it is rerun on television. In fact, a few years ago a family member bought me a DVD of this movie so that perhaps I would not be drawn to it every time it is on. The movie is *Rudy*, and the main character is played by Sean Astin (the actor who played Samwise Gamgee in the *Lord of the Rings* trilogy, likely one of the most selfless servant characters ever portrayed on film). *Rudy* has many memorable scenes, but two in particular relate to finding one's authentic voice and helping others do so. Throughout the movie Rudy's single-minded passion is Notre Dame football. (He wants to be a student there and make the football team.)

In the first scene, his friend Jim, also on the practice team, confronts Rudy as he ices his leg after a long and difficult practice. Jim tells Rudy he is making life difficult for everyone on the practice team because he is working so hard. (Rudy's hard work is a result of his passion for the team and his mission to help the team achieve its best). Jim tells Rudy he has no chance of making the team and asks why he is trying so hard. Rudy responds that he wants to help the team get ready for the game. He asks Jim why he is on the team if he does not share this mission. In sharp contrast to Rudy, who has found an inner voice that propels him to achievement, Jim admits that he is on the team to keep his father happy and willing to pay his tuition. Later,

---

52. *The 8th Habit: From Effectiveness to Greatness,* page 5.

when Rudy has doubts and threatens to quit, Jim again confronts him. Jim asks why Rudy is threatening to quit. Rudy rebuffs him, and Jim reveals that Rudy is the reason he has stayed on the team. In fact, Rudy's mission and passion have helped Jim understand his own purpose for staying on the Notre Dame football team for so long.

For me, finding my authentic voice was not as dramatic as in the movie *Rudy*. In my early career at a small firm, I had the opportunity to practice in so many different areas of the law. Not only did I discover strengths and weaknesses, I also discovered that certain areas of practice and aspects of the business were not just enjoyable, they were energizing. During this two-year period, I discovered my authentic voice—a passion for specific areas of the law and for management, along with a call to lead others.

Leadership Thought and Application

The late Stephen R. Covey, author of *The Seven Habits of Highly Effective People* and *The 8th Habit: From Effectiveness to Greatness*, is probably the leadership expert most closely associated with the concept of finding one's authentic voice. In *The 8th Habit*, Covey writes about a leader's need to find his or her voice and to inspire followers to find their voices as well. This concept applies equally to law firm and business leaders and the people they lead. But, you may ask, what exactly is my voice, and how do I find it?

Covey believes that deep within everyone is a longing for a life of meaning, purpose, and greatness. Other leadership experts might describe *voice* as a calling that compels an individual to make a meaningful contribution. For a law firm leader, finding a voice means understanding the reason he or she becomes a leader. Is it just a position? Is it just about establishing, maintaining, or exerting power over others? Is it just about control? Finding one's authentic voice may mean realizing that life can still be quite mediocre even for someone who excels in law firm management or the practice of law.

In more than 350 pages Covey explains the factors and considerations in finding and expressing one's authentic voice. I strongly recommend that every leader consider studying and being challenged by Covey's leadership model in *The 8th Habit*. As a brief study on finding an authentic voice, consider the following principles adapted from that book with application for lawyers:

Modeling. This is always the first consideration. It's about having a personal focus in your life and displaying it to others, which leads to trustworthiness. For lawyers, modeling has two factors:

1. **Having a personal vision and mission that you believe in and live.** You need to be able to answer questions like these: What do I believe? What do I see as my highest and most important value in life? What is my vision in the short term and long term? What am I truly passionate about? What are my talents, and how can I use them best to further my purpose and vision?

2. **Understanding and living the mission, vision, and values of the law firm.** The most important factor in modeling is for the leader to live up to the established values, rules, and procedures of the firm. People will not listen to anyone's voice unless it is consistent. The leader's voice will only be heard, and the leader will only be able to help others find their voices, if there is consistency between a leader's words and actions.

Pathfinding. This is the second principle. For an individual, it is about having a process to plan personal vision, values, and priorities. For the law firm, it is the necessary process of strategic planning (see Chapter 7). Covey describes a well-rounded process that includes all stakeholders. A leader should be in charge of the process of finding the organization's path, and the leader should model this process. How this leadership looks depends upon the voice of the leader, but it must be consistent with his or her life. Specifically in this unique way, the process should consider and answer the following, which are adopted from Covey's *The 8th Habit*:

1. **Market realities.** How do firm stakeholders perceive the market, including competition from local law firms and other legal service providers (both licensed and non-licensed), such as those competing through the Internet?
2. **Core competencies.** What types of practice do firm members really excel at? What areas of law and client service do they have a passion for? Is there a demand for legal services in the areas of our passion?
3. **Stakeholder wants and needs.** Very often, planning processes address strengths, weaknesses, opportunities, and threats—but only those that are external. They rarely address the wants and needs of stakeholders, which include clients as well as employees.
4. **Values.** What are the values of the law firm? Are they being used as guidelines for action?

Aligning. According to Covey, this is the third principle . It is about creating systems and structures that reinforce the core values and highest strategic priorities of the law firm. Personally, the leader commits to living out the voice and has a plan and priorities to properly define it.

The leader needs a structure of discipline that helps maintain a consistent life. This structure includes policies and procedures that keep members focused on priorities. Discipline is one of the most difficult aspects of leadership because the leader must create a proper balance between achieving short-term goals and attending to long-term priorities. Whether in the leader's personal or professional life, this discipline must

1. be created with stakeholder involvement that establishes buy-in,

2. contain a system of reward and encouragement of interdependence among firm members,
3. provide the means to establish capability to achieve results, and
4. include constant feedback to and from those carrying out the collective voice of the organization.

Empowerment. This is the final principle. It is about enabling action. Theoretically, inner passion, or voice, empowers a leader. In practice, a leader needs to make time to allow this passion to flourish. *Empowerment* has become a buzzword with different meanings, depending on a person's motives and intent. For the law firm that desires a specific and unique voice in an increasingly competitive environment, empowerment needs to be the result of the first three principles. When firm members see management acting like true leaders, living out agreed-upon values, leading the firm to a common purpose and vision, and living up to agreed-upon disciplines, they will feel and be empowered. In effect, they will find their own voices within the authentic voice of the law firm, and the leader will have helped them in that discovery.

Questions to Ponder

- Do you know your own authentic voice? What is your passion? How is that expressed through your position of leadership? Do you have your own personal mission and vision in life?
- How well do you model your authentic voice to others?
- Do you have systems or methods that help your followers align their own lives with the voice of the law firm?

Suggested Reading

Stephen R. Covey, *The 8th Habit: From Effectiveness to Greatness* (New York: Simon & Schuster, 2004).

Michael Novak, *Business as a Calling: Work and the Examined Life* (New York: Simon & Schuster, 1996).

LESSON 21 SAFETY, POWER, AND TRUST IN YOUR PRESENCE

> *Inspirational leaders are beacons of hope. They project an aura of confidence and resolve that is quite literally contagious. Churchill had this gift.... "The leader must have infectious optimism, and the determination to persevere in the face of difficulties," said Field Marshall Montgomery, a man in whom Churchill had great confidence. 'He must also radiate confidence, even when he himself is not too certain of the outcome. The final test of a leader is the feeling you have when you leave his presence after a conference. Have you a feeling of uplift and confidence?'*
>
> —Celia Sandys and Jonathan Littman[53]

During the darkest days of World War II, one person stood ready to provide the comfort and encouragement that a leader needs to supply at all times. The German planes, day after day, blitzed England with bombs and turned buildings into rubble. From the first bombing raid to the last, Winston Churchill took it upon himself to head to ground zero, stand on top of the still-smoldering ruins of English civilization, and offer encouragement to the masses. Churchill, even in the toughest of times, displayed to the British people that he had hope and confidence. He remained calm and told the truth to the British people, adding his perspective to it. He had the ability to connect with the people and galvanize them with his comforting words. In his speeches he seemed to recognize that without reassurance the people would be frightened of potential changes in their way of life and the effect of these changes on their families. As a leader, Churchill also had a team whom he led quite well through these difficult days. He insisted that those in the ranks

---

53. *We Shall Not Fail: The Inspiring Leadership of Winston Churchill,* page 174.

of leadership have a spirit of confidence and resolve during those tough times.

In law firm leadership and the practice of law, no days can ever be compared with the perilous situation faced by Great Britain in the early 1940s. At the same time, situations do arise in which similar leadership attitudes and actions need to be displayed. For me, one such event occurred just before my last year as chair of my firm's management committee. One day, my firm of twenty-five lawyers was blindsided by a blow from three partners and one associate who we thought were on the team. Two of the departing members each had twenty or more years' service as members of my firm. They asked to meet with the management committee and announced they were leaving that day to work for another firm down the street. The firm was larger, and they likely believed the move would assure greater financial security in the future. This was the first such occurrence in my leadership. As you can imagine, I learned many lessons from this situation, and one is relevant here. A person in authority who conducts himself or herself well in a time of perceived crisis will inspire a feeling of safety and trust in others. I am certainly not writing this story to brag about my ability to comfort others; it is likely one of my weakest leadership qualities. However, this situation presented the opportunity, and I found, as did other firm leaders, that our attitude, activities, and action protected the firm and provided comfort even to members who may have previously questioned my leadership abilities. I would have had no idea about how to handle such a situation had I not dedicated myself to the study of leadership over many years. Leaders who have studied leadership may find that leadership principles come to mind easily in times of crisis.

Such an experience for a midsize law firm can be very unsettling. At first I was rattled and wondered briefly whether I had done something to drive the members away. However, I did not dwell on this question. The past was over, and my partners needed to know that firm leaders would calmly develop a plan. The partners needed to hear confidence in the voices of each member of the management team so they could believe that the firm would move forward and that our financial base would be maintained. Our staff needed to be reassured that the firm was stable and that their respective positions were not in jeopardy. I found that displays of confidence and hope made others confident as well. As a leader, it was incumbent upon me to address any negativity I observed in the firm. As it turned out, the perceived crisis was an opportunity for the whole firm to come together and work as a team. Individual partners and other firm members forged relationships that some of the members of management had previously thought impossible. I believe that all of the firm owners came away from the experience stronger, closer, and with a greater appreciation for the firm as an organization.

Leadership Thought and Application

When people act as they should, in a manner worthy of their position in a firm, the positive behavior is contagious: people they follow and people they lead are also more likely to act as they should. All law firms hit bumps in the road during their organizational life, and at these times leaders must be sure that other members feel secure. A feeling of security is only possible if there is trust between and among management and members of the organization. With mutual trust, all members of the firm will feel empowered in their work for the organization, even in the most difficult of times. To help others feel secure in your presence, consider these principles:

1. **Mutual submission.** Followers are generally considered to be in submission in an organization. However, leadership itself necessitates a mutual submission of leaders and followers to each other and to the firm and its mission, vision, purposes, and objectives. Recognized universal mutual submission will inspire trust among the members of the firm.

2. **Side-by-side hierarchy.** For others to feel safety, power, and trust in your presence and leadership, all leaders and followers in the firm must have a servant mentality (see Lesson 2). Followers and leaders in the firm must have a side-by-side relationship instead of a top-down relationship. Each member within the organization provides a different type of service that focuses on achieving some part of the mission and goals of the firm. All members need to feel, and be treated as, equally valuable in the eyes of the firm and its leaders.
3. **Servant-based discipline.** If you make obedience a condition of your service as a leader, you will not create a climate of trust. You need to lead regardless of whether followers ever show trust. Trust comes as a natural result of the servant leadership you show.

Questions to Ponder

- Do the members of your firm trust you as a leader? If only partially, or conditionally, what caused the lack of trust? What can be done to repair, rebuild, or strengthen the present level of trust among members of the firm?
- Have you experienced a crisis where you or a firm member was able to create a sense of security for members in the firm? If so, what aspects of the relationships among firm members and leaders helped create this feeling of security?
- Have you experienced a crisis where fear was out of control? If so, why was that the case?
- What can you do today to put the above-stated principles into action?

Suggested Reading

Celia Sandys and Jonathan Littman, *We Shall Not Fail: The Inspiring Leadership of Winston Churchill* (New York: Penguin Group, 2003).

Seth Godin, *Linchpin: Are You Indispensable?* (New York: Penguin Group, 2010).

Chapter 4: TRUST AND AUTONOMY

Trust lies at the heart of a functioning cohesive team. Without it, teamwork is all but impossible ... trust is the confidence among team members that their peers' intentions are good, and that there is no reason to be protective or careful around the group.

—Patrick Lencioni[54]

Leaders must fully understand the two key terms *trust* and *autonomy*. Trust is a key to leadership. A leader will have no followers if others in the firm don't trust the leader. Autonomy at its most basic level is the opposite of trust. Members of an organization who trust their leader are willing to be led. Autonomy, on the other hand, is the desire to be led by no one. People who are autonomous want to make their own decisions. However, it is possible that with a climate of trust, followers can be autonomous in a way that is quite beneficial to the organization. Such autonomy is often called empowerment, and it can lead to innovative action consistent with the firm mission and strategy.

Lawyers are a unique sort. As a general rule, we desire and aggressively protect their autonomy. From the first day of class in law school, we learn to question everything. No doubt that what makes

---
54. *The Five Dysfunctions of a Team: A Leadership Fable,* page 175.

us good at what we do for clients generally makes us less trusting of others. A lack of trust makes us less able to work well as a team, because working together toward common goals requires trust. Low-trust environments, like law firms of more than one owner/partner, are replete with problems. Leaders who attempt to implement initiatives in a low-trust environment will rarely succeed, because autonomy is counter to commitment, accountability, and teamwork. The firm may organize and charge large committees and task forces charged with drafting policies and procedures that they hope will empower members, but members, who desire autonomy, will avoid spending time on the work of these committees and task forces. Finally, decision making is slowed down to such an extent that the firm becomes stagnant. Changes that do occur are late because they don't keep up with the rate of change in the community, state, and nation. The only neutralizing factor about this inability to change is that law firm members can take some comfort in the fact that (at least until recently) their primary competition is other law firms with lawyers who are just as untrusting and autonomous. With the rapid increase of nonlawyer legal service providers who do not have the decision making and control systems of typical law firms, this may no longer be true.

Given these tendencies in lawyers and law firms, can a law firm leader do anything to change this seemingly inherent and unbreakable cycle of autonomy and lack of trust? This chapter has five lessons to help the leader understand trust and deal appropriately with autonomy issues in a law firm. The first lesson explores how a leader's courage fosters an atmosphere of trust. The next lesson examines the various roles of law firm members and the attitude that each needs to contribute to a productive and positive atmosphere in the firm. The third lesson focuses on the value of diversity—including ethnicities, genders, and educational and life experiences—and how diversity in a law firm can help it achieve its mission. The fourth lesson moves into the area of penalties and rewards that can be used to encourage appropriate conduct and performance or discourage improper actions and activities. The last lesson in this chapter considers the difficult issue of dealing with conflict in the law firm. Obviously, autonomy and lack of trust may lead to conflict situations between members of the firm and management, as well as among the members themselves. The lesson includes several ways that conflict in a law firm can be used as an opportunity for leadership.

Suggested Reading

Patrick Lencioni, *The Five Dysfunctions of a Team: A Leadership Fable* (San Francisco: Jossey-Bass, 2002).

John C. Maxwell, *Everyone Communicates, Few Connect: What the Most Effective People Do Differently* (Nashville: Thomas Nelson, 2010).

LESSON 22 A LEADER'S COURAGE IS THE FOUNDATION OF TRUST

> *Some of the most brilliant, quirky, eccentric, emotionally zapped people in the world are loved by their clients, but they create living hell for everyone who has to work with them and everyone who has to lead them.*
>
> —Patrick J. McKenna and David H. Maister[55]

My favorite example of a leader having courage to act is Jimmy Stewart's portrayal of Senator Jefferson Smith in the 1939 classic movie *Mr. Smith Goes to Washington*. Smith is a newly appointed senator who feels he has no business being a senator. At the suggestion of the other senator from his state, he is encouraged to file a bill in the Senate. When the political machine boss has other ideas for the real property that is the subject of his bill, Smith is accused of trying to personally profit from the measure he has introduced. At first, Smith, under pressure to give up, considers simply walking away from the position, as he is threatened with being expelled from the Senate anyway. Instead, what occurs is one of the most impressive displays of personal courage on film. All the other senators are against him, but Smith launches a filibuster. He is attacked from every angle, but he continues until he passes out on the floor of the Senate. Finally the other senator from his state, seeing Smith's courage and considering his own participation in the scheme Smith was accused of, confesses on the Senate floor.

Law firm leaders also have the opportunity to be courageous, though in less dramatic and more mundane ways. However, some leaders seem to take the easy way out. For instance, a midsize regional law firm with a main office in a large city and several satellite offices in the same state had a major issue that was affecting one

---
55. *First among Equals: How to Manage a Group of Professionals*, page 113.

satellite's ability to contribute to the firm's mission. Each of the firm's satellites had a partner in charge. One partner at one of the satellite offices habitually wasted time by socializing with office staff, sometimes for several hours a day. Instead of confronting the socializing partner and his detrimental effect on his and the office staff's productivity, the partner in charge decided that confrontation was simply too difficult. Instead, he took action without seeking anyone else's advice: he moved the affected staff members to offices that were farther away from the socializing partner's office. The effect of these moves was an immediate increase in productivity of all those involved. However, to everyone else in the office, the move appeared to be a promotion of problem employees, because the legal assistants (secretaries) had moved to the spacious quarters usually reserved for paralegal staff who needed additional space and privacy.

Although the partner in charge's decision increased short-term productivity, his failure to address the matter directly caused a rift between him and the socializing partner, a rift that was clear to everyone else in the satellite office. The problems between these two partners were not resolved until the firm executive director traveled to the satellite office for the specific purpose of helping to negotiate a truce in the lingering conflict. He had to use intervention techniques to get the partners to talk to each other. The executive director took action because the firm was in the process of hiring a lateral attorney for that satellite office. A failure to resolve the conflict would likely have interfered with the proper integration of the new lateral hire into the firm.

This example is not from my firm, but with a few different facts it is typical of situations I have been faced with over the years and my own response as the partner in charge. Creating a policy or taking an action instead of having the courage to confront a situation head-on is easy for a person who has authority and power. I learned that if you do your best to convince a management team to support you, it is all the easier to avoid confronting a problem. I can recall specific instances where I did not have the courage to lead and found an easy way out. For me, as a transactional lawyer, the tendency to make a rule or procedure to address an issue comes as second nature. It is what I do on a day-to-day basis for my organizational clients. However, it is not necessarily the right way to handle all problems; some are better addressed directly with an individual before creating a rule or policy. By suffering through the consequences of my lack of courage in several instances during my tenure as managing partner, I learned that in the long run it is better to deal with an issue head-on.

When a policy is dictated or unilateral action has been taken to address a problem, the managing partner or management team may feel that the matter has been resolved. However, the consequences of such an action may not arise immediately. Invariably, hard feelings and resentment are harbored for a long time, not to speak of the broken trust that may never be repaired. Further, other members of the organization will be less likely to trust a leader who cannot deal fairly and personally with individual problems that arise. It takes courage to resist the temptation to take an easy way out; a type of courage that every person in a position of authority needs to be a true leader.

Leadership Thought and Application

Courage in Addressing People Problems

To repeat, trust is foundational to leadership. Additionally, a leader's courage is the foundation of trust. A difficult situation almost always calls for courageous leadership. A leader should always begin by examining the possible responses and how each might affect the firm and all of its members. The firm should be viewed as a community of people, each of whom might be affected by any decision made or action taken.

First, a leader must consider his or her motives behind a possible decision or action and ask how it will affect the other persons involved. At this point a leader must examine his or her heart, as well as the hearts of the other people involved in the difficulty. Any observable problem behavior may have deeper causes that need to be considered. An individual's internal circumstances, such as incorrect views or values, are often contributing factors to unacceptable conduct. An underlying self-centeredness or selfishness, instead of a focus on the mission of the team or firm, is often a root cause. Of course, when a leader takes action without making an initial inquiry, discovering or addressing these types of issues becomes very difficult. While investigating the underlying reasons for the unacceptable conduct, a leader will have an excellent opportunity to assure that his or her motives are just.

Second, a leader needs to determine the effect of the unacceptable conduct, as well as the proposed action or policy, on the community—the team or firm. The action of a single individual, whether it is the offending conduct or the response, will have an impact on the whole firm. People often hope or expect that the independent and autonomous actions of one person will not affect the whole organization. However, this is simply not the case, and one of the responsibilities of a leader is to instill in others the understanding that they are not on their own but that they belong to a team and the actions of one affect them all.

Disciplines of Courageous Leadership

Knowing that actions of team members—the leader and the followers—affect the team, a law firm leader must lead courageously by responding appropriately to a difficult situation and ultimately assuring that trust is not broken. Difficult situations arise not only in matters related to discipline and correction, but also when the firm faces change, decisions and adversity. Consider the following disciplines of courage that leaders need:

1. **Courage to initiate change.** Change is a given for every organization. In fact, in recent years the rate of change has been accelerating. Change used to flow like a stream, and now it is more like a rapid river. It is almost assured that a leader who decides to move a firm forward will face opposition from those who are comfortable with the status quo. Their words indicate acceptance of the change, but when the change affects them, they become resistant. To effect change, a leader must discuss the reasons for the change with those perceived to be naysayers. It is easier for a leader to move ahead either without unanimous support or without consulting others. This may not be the best decision for the long-term viability of the firm. Courage to initiate change is not just making change but also doing it in a way to achieve maximum buy-in.

2. **Courage to say no.** Just saying yes to a request or proposal is very easy. However, that may not be best for the person making the request or for the organization as a whole. In some instances, the request may require a commitment of time or effort from the management team or its leader. Because time is a finite resource, agreeing to the request may not be in the best interest of the firm. Good leaders need to have the ability to "just say no."

3. **Courage to stand up to others.** At times, a leader is faced with a request or difficult issue where those involved are simply unpleasant to deal with. In these cases, the easy way out is to simply not deal with the situation and hope that it will go away on its own. If it is a situation where someone has been hurt in some way, a leader might hope that the wounds would heal in time. The more difficult the players, the more tempting it is to turn your eyes away and pray the issue goes away. In almost every such situation, it is best to

address the issue appropriately, giving consideration to the commitment to community that every organization needs.

4. **Courage to admit you are wrong.** It is difficult for anyone to admit he or she is wrong. It is more difficult for those in the legal profession. Lawyers are generally trained to argue, sometimes for people who seem to have no real argument in their favor. Lawyers often perceive that admitting they are wrong is demeaning or beneath them. However, leadership principles are universal. If you cannot admit that you are wrong, you will break trust with those you desire to lead. There is just no way around it.

Questions to Ponder

- Are you a courageous leader? Whatever your answer, think of a time when you faced a difficult situation with an individual. Were you willing to deal with it face-to-face before dealing with it more publicly—for example, by creating a rule or policy? If you did not handle the situation well, what could you have done differently? If the result was positive, what contributed to that outcome?
- Do you view your team or firm as a community? As a concept, what does this mean to you? How does this concept guide your actions as you address day-to-day issues?
- Which of the four disciplines of Courageous Leadership is most difficult for you? Why is that the case, and what can you do to address this difficulty?

Suggested Reading

Patrick J. McKenna and David H. Maister, *First among Equals: How to Manage a Group of Professionals* (New York: Simon & Schuster, 2002).

Dale Carnegie, *How to Win Friends and Influence People* (New York: Simon & Schuster, 1936).

LESSON 23 THE VARYING ROLES AND RELATIONSHIPS OF MEMBERS OF A LAW FIRM

Winning the power to lead professionals is no easy task. Before a leader can be accepted, let alone succeed, autonomous professionals must agree to be influenced by that person.

—David H. Maister[56]

In professional football, when I think of the greatest players on offense, generally I think of individuals like Joe Montana, Barry Sanders, or Jim Brown. However, on defense it is usually more difficult for an objective person to select the greatest of all time. On offense, most people (even football novices) can differentiate between the quarterback and the running back and can generally easily identify a team leader. On defense, it is much more difficult, as the average fan generally mixes up the positions of guard and tackle or the position of safety and cornerback. Usually there is not an identifiable individual player, but a team. The greatest pro football defense in history is said to have been (per ESPN's website) the 1976 Pittsburgh Steelers. The defensive team was collectively known as the Steel Curtain. Though there is one person from that group of players who is more famous than the others (Mean Joe Green), the fame was likely created just as much by his nickname and a Coca-Cola commercial as by his exemplary play on the field. In the last nine games of the 1976 season, this team defense gave up a total of only twenty-eight points. Eight defensive players from this team (and there are only eleven defensive players on the field at any one time) made the 1976 Pro Bowl. The legendary coach of the Steelers, Chuck Noll, in describing his players, said:

---

56. *True Professionalism: The Courage to Care about Your People, Your Clients, and Your Career,* page 65.

> The single most important thing we had in the Steelers of the 1970s was an ability to work together. The thing that stuck out was we had a lot of people who didn't worry about what somebody else did. If someone else was having a tough time on a particular day, they reached down and got it up a little more. They got the thing done. Whatever they had to do, they did to win. There was never a reason to let down . . . Right now you hear about teamwork and it's defined as 50-50, and that is a falsehood. There's no such thing as 50-50. You do whatever you have to do as part of the team. You may have to carry somebody . . . I can't tell you how much you gain, how much progress you can make, by working together as a team, by helping one another. You get much more done that way. If there's anything the Steelers of the '70s epitomized, I think it was that teamwork.[57]

Regardless of the fact that outsiders may not recognize the names of the various positions or the contribution each member has on defense, it is understanding the roles and relationships of all team members that enables a team to work well together and helps a coach be a successful leader.

This simple fact of teamwork is also what makes law firms work so well. A lack of understanding and acknowledgment of the roles and contributions of each member of a law firm will be a significant contributing factor to organizational and leadership failure.

A Boston law firm that seems to get this concept of understanding roles and teamwork is Exemplar Law, LLC (which is a part of the professional services team of Exemplar Company; see www.exemplarcompanies.com). According to Exemplar's website, the firm environment is one where people work together in a "collaborative, collegial environment, sharing ideas and experiences while leveraging diversity of thought, openness and individuality." Certainly this claim could not be true unless those who lead the firm, and those who are members, understand and appreciate the

---

57. Gerry Dulac, "On His Day in Spotlight, Noll Cites Others for Success," *Pittsburgh Post-Gazette*, August 1, 1993. Chuck Noll's comments upon induction into the Pro Football Hall of Fame.

contribution of each member to the overall work and mission of the firm. Although the substantive work at this firm may not be easy, the description of the environment as found on the firm's website suggests that every team member possesses the qualities espoused. This would have to mean that leadership of the firm understands and supports the role of each firm member. According to consultant David Maister, Christopher Marston, the firm's founder, describes the team atmosphere as follows:

> A "No Grinch" teamwork approach. Marston says on his blog, "You cannot buy a position at our firm with your book of business. In fact, we have turned several of them away. We want everyone to work together to achieve success."[58]

Leadership Thought and Application

The failure of a leader to understand the role, and properly recognize the contributions, of each firm member will negatively impact the ability of a leader to accomplish success in his or her leadership. In every leadership role, whether it is a partner in a known and established position of authority or simply a new associate with some ability to have an impact on the decisions, actions, and conduct of others, there is an opportunity to lead through influence; and influence, if a person has it, is what leadership is really all about. The role that you play as a leader will vary depending upon the situation you are in within the firm. So regardless of your job description or position, it is first and foremost important to have an understanding of the organizational chart of the law firm, who reports to whom, and what function each person primarily has. Given this information, make a commitment to use your leadership role to better accomplish the mission of the law firm team.

---

58. David Maister, "An Innovative Law Firm," *Passion, People and Principles* (blog), April 2006, http://davidmaister.com/articles/2/98/

Leadership without authority. If you do not have a traditional leadership position within the firm (you are not the managing partner, on an executive committee, the chair of a practice group, etc.), then consider committing to the following principles to guide your actions:

1. **Respect authority.** In every law firm there are established lines of authority. In most firms, as well as other professional organizations, the lines of authority can be blurred at times. A law firm with a large group of owners commonly has associates, paralegals, legal assistants, and staff who are directly supervised by specific individuals or teams (perhaps through a practice group) of owners (partners). There can tend to be a kind of protection granted by partners to those persons seen as directly under them. This protection can lead to a sense of security in regard to other systems of authority created in the firm for global concerns (such as management, billing, technology, payroll, and administration). This sense of security can result in a tendency to show a lack of respect for those who are not direct supervisors. Respect is not just outward behavior, but it needs to be genuine and from the heart. Backbiting after outward compliance is not an example of respect for authority.

2. **Have a true desire to render service to others.** A desire to render service is not just the desire to get a paycheck or some quid pro quo, but a desire to take actions in good faith; ones that are truly for the benefit of others and not self. If leadership is about influence, and trust is the foundation of influence, volunteering to help another in the time of need, without the expectation of any glory or compensation, will certainly mean volumes in your development of leadership potential in the organization.

Leadership with authority. If you do have a recognized position of leadership in the firm, consider committing to the following principles that should apply to all of your actions:

1. **Respect those who are not in authority.** It is very easy for someone in a position of leadership to forget that the position is not one of special perks and benefits for the leader. It seems to be human nature to desire to be loved and respected as a leader, not understanding that these desires come to everyone, regardless of position. An exalted position in a law firm should not be seen as an exalted position in life. Further, a leader must see each position as simply a role within the well-oiled machine, which is the law firm. Different positions may have different pay, benefits, and responsibilities, but all members of the firm team need to be given the type of respect that they not only deserve, but which the organization deserves to give them, such that they are encouraged and enthused in their work. (When viewed objectively, job responsibilities may be more or less important, but when viewed relationally they are equally important.)

2. **Desire to render service to others, regardless of whether they are in positions of authority.** Service to others, including those usually recognized as subordinates, can take many different forms. Service rendered to all members of the team will reap untold benefits for a leader who desires to experience joy in his or her position, as well as see to the achievement of success in the mission of the organization. Practically, service might take the form of providing opportunities for staff members in their professional development, such as training and education in areas they might grow into in the future, or treating them fairly and speaking the truth to them in a manner that shows true interest and respect.

3. **Display objectively appropriate action or conduct.** Action taken by a person in a position of authority should

not be seen as threatening of others. Action should be taken only if it does not cause fear of domination in the person whom it affects or concerns. Certainly all organizations need appropriate policies and procedures, and members of an organization need to be held accountable. At the same time, team members should not see the leader as being so overbearing that failure in their work is assured.

4. **Do not show partiality.** A leader should always focus on the organization as a team, and every member, regardless of the possible perceived relative importance of the task he or she performs, should be respected and treated fairly. Leaders should not take any action that might be construed as being based on a unique set of rules or policies for different levels of members of the team, unless the standard has some identifiable business purpose behind its application. Favoritism is not such a reason.

5. **Give affirmation and feedback on a regular basis.** A leader should define his or her position in authority as one that seeks to assure that followers are successful. Actions should only be taken with this firmly in mind. Response to conduct of followers should not be given for reasons of favoritism or retribution, but instead be gauged to assure individual and organizational success.

Questions to Ponder

- Do you show favoritism in your leadership? If so, how? If not, are there times when you assign to some staff members tasks that you feel are beneath the work of a lawyer?
- Is there a hierarchy of positions in your law firm? Can you draw a diagram of it? Is it a hierarchy that can be supported logically for the greater good and future success of the firm, or is it based on archaic views of the legal profession?

- Of all of the principles to guide a leader's action listed above, which do you struggle with the most? Which come naturally to you? Why?

Suggested Reading

David H. Maister, *True Professionalism: The Courage to Care about Your People, Your Clients, and Your Career* (New York: Simon & Schuster, 1997).

John C. Maxwell, *Winning with People: Discover the People Principles That Work for You Every Time* (Nashville: Thomas Nelson, 2004).

LESSON 24 DIVERSITY AND GENDER

[D]iversity has rapidly made the transition from a necessary evil to a competitive advantage for the businesses that manage it effectively—an advantage that no successful leader today can ignore.

—R. Roosevelt Thomas Jr.[59]

When I think of the most diverse areas in the country, I usually think of places like Miami, San Francisco, and New York—big cities with large populations, cities that have had a large influx of people over many years. However, I probably live in one of the most diverse places in the country: Asheville, North Carolina. It has not always been that way, but it is now. It is a large melting pot of different kinds of people: people who look different from each other, people who have different views on religion, sexual preference, and politics, people who speak differently, and people who have different views on economic matters. Asheville is a small city on a plateau within the mountains of western North Carolina. It is the largest community west of Charlotte and is surrounded by small towns that do not seem to share the diversity that it enjoys.

When one thinks of the South, a willingness to embrace diversity is rarely the first thought that comes to mind. In fact, until very recently, some organizations refused to have large meetings in southern locations where the Confederate flag could be or was displayed, or in places that seemed divided by racism. But Asheville, North Carolina, has undergone continual change, as has my law firm.

When I came to the firm in 1988, the organization was a homogeneous organization. Yes, we did have a few woman lawyers, and all of the staff members were women, but management and ownership were primarily white men. As an Italian American from the

---

59. *The Leader of the Future 2: Visions, Strategies, and Practices for the New Era,* page 47.

Northeast, I probably accounted for the only diversity in the firm. At the time, no staff or lawyers were African American, and, if I remember correctly, everyone was Christian. Much has changed in twenty-three years. In that time, we have become much more diverse in many ways, and I find that our diversity has pretty much matched the diversity in Asheville. To some extent, I see the changes as circumstantial or coincidental. At the same time, I can tell that prior firm leaders were open to new thoughts and ideas. In my view we are far from perfect in regard to diversity, but, thanks to the excellent leadership of the previous leaders of my firm, I believe that I have learned key principles for making diversity and inclusiveness a priority in any law firm.

Leadership Thought and Application

Stand up to bias and prejudice in the workplace. Even with all of the recent changes in law firms in the area of diversity, much more can and should be done. Many firms seem to have embraced the appearance of diversity, but some still seem to tolerate underlying bias and prejudice. If you want to be a leader, one of your primary tasks is addressing any underlying bias or prejudice within the firm. As previously mentioned, typical law firm compensation systems tend to reward objective financial considerations and not activities and conduct that are more difficult to quantify, even though they provide great (or greater) value to the law firm in achieving its mission. Such compensation systems work against a leader who is attempting to address bias, prejudice, or discrimination.

As a leader, regardless of those factors within the law firm that tend to work against you, it is critical that you take a stand when necessary. I believe two basic principles apply: first, don't join in, and second, speak up.

A true leader knows how to respond to bias or discrimination in the workplace. Leaders must address actions that are obviously inappropriate or actionable, as well as hurtful words and deeds even if they do not occur in the presence of the people whom they offend. The most likely offenses are insensitive comments or jokes. A leader must know when to not join the comments and when to take specific action and address the inappropriate conduct or speech at an appropriate time with the offender. To quote the leadership expert John Maxwell, "People do what people see." If a firm leader tells offensive jokes or laughs at them, he or she tells everyone—the offenders and those who might find the conduct offensive—that this type of conduct is acceptable.

Professionalism, diversity, and tolerance help achieve mission. A leader also needs to recognize that professionalism, diversity, and tolerance work together to achieve the mission and vision of the firm. Mission and vision almost always include a statement about serving clients in the most professional, effective, and efficient manner possible. To do this, especially in an ever-changing world, you need access to the broadest spectrum of views possible. The more the firm embraces diversity, the better able the members will be to serve clients whose personal and business interests must fit in an increasingly diverse world. Even in very busy legal practices, leaders need an organized and effective program for embracing diversity, a program that is intentional, perpetual, and comprehensive.

1. **Intentional.** Diversity does not just happen. Most people tend to flock around those whom they are like—those with common characteristics, life experiences, and features. Law firms that focus on only having members who fit the "culture" of the Firm, may miss the opportunity that diversity brings. The Firm may also be working counter to any intentional diversity program in place. An analysis of this tendency is beyond the scope of this book, but suffice it to say that because of this tendency a leader must understand that achieving some measure of diversity requires leadership, planning, and well-organized execution.

2. **Perpetual.** An emphasis on diversity is not a time-limited program. Just as the means of achieving a firm's mission and purpose may change from year to year, so will the means by which diversity goals and objectives are achieved. And just like mission and purpose, the diversity program must not be limited in duration.

3. **Comprehensive.** A leader needs to have a plan that covers the whole organization, not just its lawyers. It is crucial that all lawyers and staff understand that firm leaders are committed to diversity within the organization and that they have zero tolerance for intolerance.

Think beyond traditional diversity. What do we mean by *traditional diversity?* Traditionally, programs are geared toward diversity in the areas of gender, race, and religion. More recently, for some, *traditional diversity* is interpreted to include sexual preference and ethnicity. A leader who believes diversity will contribute to the firm's success needs to think of diversity more broadly. The most effective law firm diversity programs will also consider, for example, areas such as the following:

1. **Educational experience.** Is it really necessary that every lawyer is a graduate of a Tier 1 law school? Some well-qualified and promising candidates are from other law schools where the emphasis is not as much on traditional academics as it is on producing practice-ready lawyers.

2. **Life experience.** At one time the standard candidate went directly from high school to a college or university and finally to law school, with very little time to gain life experiences, other than those gained in the course of growing up. In addition to lawyers with this traditional educational path, firms may want to consider members who have had nonlaw experiences' because they can help make the firm well-rounded.

3. **Outside interests.** In North Carolina, it seems that everyone is interested in college football and basketball. From December through March, Monday morning conversations are always about basketball. As a season ticket holder, I can vouch for the entertainment value of following a college through the ACC. At the same time, a firm is missing something if everyone has the identical interests. When lawyers and professional staff share diverse outside interests, they can help bring firm members together.

Obviously, interviewers must follow the law when investigating and considering candidates for open positions. However, to the extent that a firm can include these aspects of diversity as well as more traditional aspects in their hiring decisions, the firm will be more representative of society and therefore generally more able to address the needs of all of its clients.

Questions to Ponder

- Do you believe that those whose background or experience is different from yours feel comfortable in your Firm? If so, what makes you think so? If not, why not?
- Would the answer to the preceding question be the same if these people listened to all the members' conversations, including jokes?
- Are you willing to lead your firm on an exploration of diversity as a way of life? If not, what is holding you back, and what can be done about it?

Suggested Reading

Frances Hesselbein and Marshall Goldsmith, eds., *The Leader of the Future 2: Visions, Strategies, and Practices for the New Era* (San Francisco: Jossey-Bass, 2006).

Michael Schutzler, *Inspiring Excellence: A Path to Exceptional Leadership* (Bothell, WA: Book Publishers Network, 2009).

LESSON 25 RULES AND PROCEDURES: CARROTS AND STICKS

> *The executive called all his key staff members together to tell them of his dissatisfaction and to introduce to them the consultant he had hired to help shape the place up. True to his style, he ended the meeting by warning his staff, "Any of you who don't shape up in the next thirty days are going to be fired."*
>
> *After the meeting the shocked consultant privately coached the executive to move away from ruling by fear and to substitute positive motivation instead. Trying to follow this advice, the executive called another meeting the very next day. It was a short meeting during which he said, 'I'm going to try changing my leadership style, so I want you to disregard what I said yesterday. Instead, I want to assure each of you that anyone who shapes up in the next thirty days will be able to keep his job!'*
>
> —Jim Lundy[60]

In the carrot-and-stick model of leadership, the ultimate example is the discipline system used by the military. These models are also common in international diplomacy, where they are usually intended to coerce or threaten nations into compliance with standards that a more powerful nation values. Carrots (incentives) are usually economic or military aid or a reduction of trade barriers, and sticks (consequences) usually include the threat of military intervention or economic sanctions. Politically, the carrot-and-stick model is controversial. One side believes that carrots are not effective, but sticks are a time-tested method of achieving results. The other side argues that even if sticks gain compliance, they harm the international image of the powerful nation and may lead to extreme distrust.

---

60. *Lead, Follow, or Get Out of the Way*, pages 63–64.

Even though the stakes may not be as high as in international relations between nation states, the basics of the international carrot-and-stick approach may also apply in a law firm. Misuse of punishment tends to paralyze law firm leaders because while they may gain compliance, they do so at the risk of losing trust and respect. Without consequence for improper action, a carrot system may have a positive effect on some, but it may not motivate the firm's most autonomous members.

In my experience, a leadership team and a firm COO need to motivate members in many different areas that are related to achieving the firm's mission. Perhaps you have thought about how to deal with some of the following day-to-day problems and performance issues:

- nonexempt staff member tardy to work on a regular basis
- nonexempt employee working unapproved overtime
- failure to record time on a daily basis
- failure to finalize bills as required each month
- failure to gain approval for overtime of supervised staff
- failure to comply with billing policies regarding discounting, write-offs, and write-downs
- inadequate billed hours or any other commitment not being met
- failure to attend required meetings (practice group, staff, monthly lawyer meetings, or other firm committee)
- failure to fulfill nonbillable commitments

Leadership Thought and Application

A focus on orderly policies and procedures is good, but too great a focus on rules can lead to missed opportunities. In addition, law firm leaders should consider a good mix of incentives and consequences. Rewards and punishments should generally apply only to conduct, not results. Results are achieved through action that targets the mission, goals, and objectives that were established collectively. When results are the sole basis for rewards, some members of the firm will be rewarded because they are lucky. Alternatively, when a member who is unable to meet financial goals or other objectives in spite of his or her actions in support of the firm mission, goals, and objectives, a penalty may seem unfair or cause the firm member to despair. As a result, the penalty will not motivate the member.

Law firm leaders need to be very careful about their rules and procedures, especially those that carry benefits or consequences to firm members. There are a few principles to consider when drafting and applying carrot-and-stick incentives.

The binding nature of legalism. Generally a firm member who complies with rules and procedures feels good about adherence. But law firm leaders should discourage complacency and encourage members to excel beyond the desired standard and in doing so live up to their potential. Rules and procedures need to be explained to members as a floor (or minimum standard) and clearly not a ceiling. These standards are analogous to the Rules of Professional Conduct for lawyers. Compliance is the minimal conduct permitted, but certainly lawyers should strive at all times to exceed the minimum. Leaders who focus too much on conduct and compliance and the accompanying incentives and punishments may inadvertently create ceilings for behavior. As a result, everyone in the firm may try to look good to each other by meeting but not exceeding the standard. Leaders also need to make sure that firm policies and procedures allow them to use discretion in situations when the failure to comply is ultimately for the betterment of the firm. Certainly leaders do not want to be perceived as inconsistent in applying rules; but this flexibility, when given and understood by firm owners, may actually allow individual members of the firm to reach new heights in performance.

Rules and procedures may stifle vision. Rules and procedures can work against a law firm achieving its mission and vision because living up to the standards in the rules and procedures causes members to be more inwardly focused (on themselves) and less outwardly focused (on clients or fellow members of the firm). Rules and procedures are usually focused inward, concentrating on the conduct of the individual firm members. Unless leaders narrowly craft rules and procedures with an outward focus on client service, applying the rules and procedures can take the joy out of practicing law and achieving the firm mission and vision.

Rules and procedures need to be diverse. Avoid stating rules and procedures in a *do not* format. Rules that forbid behavior can actually challenge people to break or work around the spirit or intent behind the wording. Lawyers, who are naturally autonomous, are especially likely to find ways around rules. Lawyers who desire to get around a rule or procedure frequently use their excellent command of the language to find technical flaws in the wording, even though everyone in the organization knows the desired application and intent of the rule. The word *don't* can make those who have to comply feel that their compliance is causing them to miss out on something. Though *don't* rules may be necessary to set boundaries, a leader can instead emphasize a *do* rule to encourage behavior that is incompatible with the prohibited behavior. For instance, these law firm rules use a more positive means to communicate:

- A client intake policy and procedure that encourages partners to accept certain client matters within specified parameters without prior consent may be preferable to a policy that prohibits all client matters without prior consent. Such a rule might apply to personal injury contingent work, which requires outlays of at-risk expense monies. This is an example of a policy that contains a *don't* followed by a *do*.
- A partner expenditure policy that allows each partner to buy equipment that he or she reasonably believes is necessary for

practice may be better than a policy that requires approval of all purchases. For example, a partner may make purchases of up to a certain dollar limit and within an annual (or quarterly) budget without approval. As a part of the policy, each partner would be required to let the other partners know of the expenditure within a month after purchase, giving information about the type of equipment that was purchased and how it is being used in the practice of law, including recommendation on whether the purchase is something others should consider. The firm may still have a prohibitory *don't* rule, but it can emphasize an innovative *do* instead.

Questions to Ponder

- How does your firm hold members accountable for compliance with rules and procedures? Are most of your consequences benefits or punishments? Can you name any incentives that have worked in your firm? If so, why did they work so well?
- Have you found that any of your firm members become complacent when they hit or achieve established standards? What types of incentives might cause greater initiative to exceed goals and objectives?
- Do most of your rules and procedures prohibit some type of conduct? Name a few of these rules and procedures. Is there any way that they can be rewritten so they are empowering instead of prohibitive?

Suggested Reading

Jim Lundy, *Lead, Follow, or Get Out of the Way* (San Diego: Slawson Communications, 1986).

Michael Feiner, *The Feiner Points of Leadership: The 50 Basic Laws That Will Make People Want to Perform Better for You* (New York: Time Warner Book Group, 2004).

LESSON 26 DEALING WITH CONFLICT

Leaders who can traverse boundaries have always been vital to civilization, but today the need for this leadership capacity is even more urgent and widespread. . . . We simply cannot manage a whole company, a whole community—and certainly not a whole planet—with leaders who identify with only one part. . . . There is no denying that the potential for dangerous, destructive conflict is real. How we choose to respond to this conflict is an act of leadership. We need a new model of leadership that puts conflict at the center, as an essential test of leadership.

—Mark Gerzon[61]

Conflict is an inevitable part of leadership. If you are a leader and do not perceive any conflict in your law firm (or if you have not identified that conflict), you most likely don't have any followers either. The fight-or-flight response to conflict is human nature, but rarely is either approach constructive. Neither is another common approach—ignoring problems until they become critical issues that affect the whole organization. When this occurs, conflict may have evolved into crisis.

Instead of addressing problems head-on, the managing partner in one firm often created logical policies to address members' improper conduct. By not dealing with issues head-on, the managing partner avoided directly confronting members or the problems they caused. The response was to fight and flee at the same time. The leader's avoidance was a way to flee the problem, and the offending members considered the established policies as personal public attacks. Interestingly, none of the policies ever singled out an individual firm

---

61. *Leading through Conflict: How Successful Leaders Transform Differences into Opportunities*, pages 3–4.

member, and all of the policies and procedures would be in the best interest of just about any law firm. The problem was that the policies and procedures were created soon after undesirable conduct, and specific firm members perceived them as public criticism. In fact, some even e-mailed counterattacks that were written in such a way that the entire firm could identify the wrongdoers. The failure to properly communicate policies created even further bad will between the leader and those members of the firm guilty of improper conduct.

Leadership Thought and Application

In the book *The Peacemaker*,[62] Ken Sande identifies three categories of response to human conflict: flee, fight, or conciliation. Typical flee responses include physically leaving to avoid conflict, denying conflict, or ignoring it. Typical fight responses might be argument, assault, or litigation. For a leader in a law firm, conciliation is negotiating or mediating the conflict. Consider the following when addressing conflict in a conciliatory manner:

1. **Communication.** To the extent possible, avoid using e-mail to communicate difficult messages. Instead consider contacting the players personally as the first course of action, even though—like other leadership responsibilities—it can be time-consuming. Depending on the subject of the controversy, it may be necessary to consult members of the management team. Generally, however, avoid discussing the matter with nonessential parties to limit the possibility of gossip. The purpose is not to keep secrets from fellow owners but to retain the trust of those involved, because resolution of the issue is the top priority in mediation.

2. **Motive.** When negotiating, a leader must always keep the best interests of the firm and the parties in the controversy

---

62. *The Peacemaker 2nd Edition: A Biblical Guide to Resolving Personal Conflict,* 2nd ed., Chapter 1.

as a priority. The leader should strive to keep a positive attitude that communicates a desire to help, rehabilitate, and enable others to achieve success. Maintaining trust and resolving the issue depends on communicating this attitude to the people involved.

3. **Confrontation.** Confrontation is not about argument, power, and force; it is about discussion and brainstorming positive resolution for all concerned. In this situation the confrontation is a collaborative effort. Initially a leader should communicate personally and directly with those involved to gather facts and see if a quick resolution might be possible. If any party in the conflict is not cooperative in the effort to find resolution, the leader should involve one or two other trusted advisors (perhaps someone who is trusted by those involved) and attempt to gain resolution. Finally, if the parties still cannot resolve the conflict, the matter should be resolved by the highest and most appropriate governing body of the firm. Depending upon the size of the firm, that might be a managing partner, management committee, or, in the largest firms a team or committee created to resolve such matters.

   Obviously in a smaller firm conflict resolution might only be a two-step process. Depending upon the circumstances, this last step might be a direct intervention in which the leaders insist upon certain changes in conduct for the good of the organization. This type of process is one that needs much investigation, study, and consideration before being implemented. In addition, all members of the management team need to fully support the proposed action to be taken, especially if a partner is involved in the conflict. Otherwise the process is almost certain to fail. Additional information about the relationship between communication, collaboration, and effective conflict resolution is available at Stewart Levine's website Resolution Works and on his blog *Resolu-*

tionary Works (http://resolutionworks.com/resolution_works_blog/). Articles and blog posts specifically address communication and the importance of effective listening in resolution of conflict.

Questions to Ponder

- Can you think of a time when you used e-mail for a difficult message or to resolve a conflict and the matter escalated into a controversy or crisis? If so, what means of communication would have been more effective?
- Do you always have the best intentions toward the persons involved in conflict when you are negotiating? Do you tend to pick one side over another before you have heard all sides? If so, do you think that this tendency affects your ability to find the best possible solution to the conflict?
- Has your management team created a procedure for dealing with conflict in the firm? Have you ever had to have an intervention type of meeting with members of the firm involved in conflict? If so, did the process work? If not, do you believe that such a process might work when conflict seems irreconcilable?

Suggested Reading

Mark Gerzon, *Leading through Conflict: How Successful Leaders Transform Differences into Opportunities* (Boston: Harvard Business School Press, 2006).

Ken Sande, *The Peacemaker: A Biblical Guide to Resolving Personal Conflict*, 2nd ed. (Grand Rapids, MI: Baker Books, 1997).

Chapter 5
LEADERSHIP IN PRACTICE: CLIENT RELATIONS

> *Connecting with customers is about substance, not style—creating a more compelling environment to do business, whatever business you're in. In a competitive environment defined by too much choice and too many look-alike choices, it doesn't take all that much creativity to be memorable—to be different enough in your marketplace that your customers find you hard to forget.*
>
> —William C. Taylor and Polly LaBarre[63]

As lawyers, what we provide to our clients on a day-to-day basis, disguised as legal services, can be summed up in one word: leadership. The practice of law is influencing clients to make the right decisions—for example, decisions about how to negotiate a business transaction or whether to settle or litigate a controversy. Obviously, providing this type of leadership is very satisfying. Lawyer leaders should understand why.

First, serving others through leadership is a privilege and a joy. The more you do for others, the more personal satisfaction you will have. To give of yourself to others is one of the high callings of our profession.

---

63. *Mavericks at Work: Why the Most Original Minds in Business Win*, pages 157–158.

Second, leading clients is an opportunity for the lawyer to develop leadership skills. Perhaps that is part of the reason why our work is called a practice; with each case or matter, we develop and grow. Leading clients allows us to demonstrate what can be done through service and to serve as a model to others in our law firms.

Third, leadership is a blessing to both the client and the lawyer. The act of service benefits the person rendering it. Service to others may indirectly be repaid with service to the lawyer. Obviously, this is a result and not the reason for our service to others.

It is the duty of a law firm leader to recognize that leadership is an important part of what a law firm does. When members of the firm develop their leadership abilities, they are more able to help the firm achieve its mission and purpose. Leading a law firm is leading an organization of leaders. The two lessons in this chapter focus on how those in leadership positions can help individual law firm members be good leaders. The first lesson examines the lawyer-client relationship and the personal traits and characteristics that will help a lawyer be a better leader to clients. The second lesson describes some of the ways that lawyers can learn to be better leaders.

Suggested Reading
William C. Taylor and Polly LaBarre, *Mavericks at Work: Why the Most Original Minds in Business Win* (New York: Harper-Collins, 2006).

David H. Maister, *True Professionalism: The Courage to Care about Your People, Your Clients, and Your Career* (New York: Simon & Schuster, 1997).

LESSON 27 INFLUENCING CLIENTS—LEADERSHIP AS THE KEY ROLE OF A LAWYER

You know, it is often overlooked that the person who really gained the most was the Good Samaritan who rendered service, not the person who received it. I think the real lesson of the parable is that we benefit most when we help a neighbor in need.

—Dick Wirthlin (quoting Ronald Reagan)[64]

We need leaders we can trust. Leaders we can believe in. Leaders who are invested in the long-term success of their followers, our communities, our nation, and the world. Most of all, we need leaders whose concerns extend well beyond their own material possessions, golden parachutes, and status at the country club.

—Jeremie Kubicek[65]

The most memorable scene in the movie *A Few Good Men* is when Tom Cruise's character, Lieutenant Kaffee, confronts Jack Nicholson's character, Colonel Jessup, in the final court scene and gets him to admit on the witness stand that he ordered the by then infamous code red. Though this scene is the one that moviegoers recall most frequently—and which some fans can recite word for word—a different scene, earlier in the movie, depicts a lawyer who clearly does not understand what's important to his client. As a result he is incapable of client leadership at that point in his representation. In the scene, Lieutenant Kaffee is alone with his client, Corporal Dawson, and questions Dawson's definition of what is right. Kaffee tries to

---

64. *The Greatest Communicator: What Ronald Reagan Taught Me about Politics, Leadership, and Life*, page 224.
65. *Leadership Is Dead: How Influence Is Reviving It*, page 42.

use guilt to influence his client as he argues that his client's influence over his codefendant will ultimately send the codefendant to prison. The end of the scene underscores Kaffee's weakness as a leader. His client, a man who would rather die than breach military protocol, puts his hands in his pockets instead of properly saluting Kaffee.

Contrast the lack of influence that Tom Cruise's character has in that scene with Cruise's scene in the movie *The Firm*, where his character, Mitch McDeere, meets a client of his senior partner in the Cayman Islands. Through slick talk and breadth of knowledge in tax law, he convinces the client (with the addition of a vulgar analogy) to make a tax decision in the client's personal best interest. Sticking to the Tom Cruise theme, perhaps the relationship Cruise's character has with his client at the end of *Jerry Maguire* is closer to the special relationship of influence a leader should strive for, one of complete trust and loyalty brought about through service and sacrifice.

I prefer, however, an example of client influence that is personal to me, and is both real and honorable. My partner Lou Bissette is the epitome of the trusted advisor—one that every lawyer tries to emulate in each lawyer-client relationship but rarely achieves. Lou is a public servant extraordinaire. He has been the mayor of Asheville, North Carolina, and has received almost every award for dedicated public service that is given in our community. I have observed Lou in many different situations, and his refined leadership skills allow him to effectively influence others in community activities and in activities for my own law firm. Lou was a member of the management committee I chaired for twelve years, and without question he was the most significant leader in the firm during that time. Through many years of study and trial and error, I have learned many basic leadership skills. One of these is how to identify other members of a leadership team with a unique ability to influence others. Identifying Lou with a unique ability to influence others was easy. I knew that without his prior support or acquiescence, I would have a very difficult time achieving group buy-in or success with an initiative.

Most important, however, Lou is an excellent leader of clients. Because of the changes in the profession in the recent past, it seems to be impossible to practice law (especially in some of the areas of law that have become more of a commodity) without an ability to lead clients. Richard Susskind, in his book *The End of Lawyers?: Rethinking the Nature of Legal Services*,[66] talks about a type of "bespoke," or customized and engaged, counsel that few clients are still willing to pay for, though they want and expect it. It is this same type of counsel that many lawyers believe they provide, though the opposite is likely true. Lou, however, is truly at a bespoke level of client service. Those who have been privileged to have him service their legal needs find in him a true trusted advisor. My friend and partner Lou Bissette not only provides competent technical legal service but also understands that the lawyer's role in a lawyer-client relationship is truly one of leadership. Such leadership is possible because clients trust him. The trusting relationship is a result of careful listening, empathy, and projecting an attitude of genuine concern—never that clients are just files to be worked.

Leadership Thought and Application

Being a lawyer is more than simply counting how many files have been handled, how much money has been collected, or how many hours have been billed. For a lawyer who desires to be a client's trusted advisor, the most important role is that of leader, and this role provides a lawyer with the greatest satisfaction when representing a client. Client leadership is based on trust—trust that the lawyer has the client's best interests at heart and is willing to serve in a manner that provides the greatest benefit to the client. Establishing and maintaining a leadership role with clients is similar to establishing and

---

66. Richard Susskind, *The End of Lawyers?: Rethinking the Nature of Legal Services* (New York: Oxford University Press, 2010).

maintaining a leadership role in other situations. Consider these ideas about leadership in the lawyer-client relationship:

Close business relationship. As previously stated, leadership is about influence. A true leader influences others, and a lawyer leader influences clients in a positive and productive manner. Influence requires trust, and trust is a result of establishing a relationship. Without trust, a client may do what the lawyer advises for other reasons—a feeling of fear, a recommendation from a friend, or the reputation of the lawyer. But true leadership, the kind where a client is actually influenced and truly believes in the lawyer as a trusted advisor, only comes with relationship. To establish relationship, the lawyer must see the client as more than one more file in a stack that needs attention. Consider a movie scene portraying a doctor-patient relationship in which a doctor objectively discusses a patient's prognosis with other medical professionals—perhaps even discussing the chances of death—in front of the patient. In the lawyer-client relationship, the client can likewise pick up an arrogant or insensitive attitude on the part of the lawyer. Clients know when their lawyers are simply going through the motions to get another matter completed. This type of perceived attitude or work ethic works against establishing or maintaining a leadership relationship. To maintain a leadership relationship with clients, lawyers need to avoid these common pitfalls:

1. **Lack of Timeliness.** A key relationship destroyer is promising a deadline and missing it. In this area of practice, always under-promise and over-perform. Be on time or early.

2. **Lack of Communication.** Unreturned phone calls and lack of information are relationship killers. Keep clients informed about the status of their matters.

3. **Lack of Availability.** All lawyers need to balance the need to be available to clients with the need to accomplish their other work. That stated, if a lawyer wants to have influence, the client must feel that the lawyer is available to him or her.

Legal competency. Leadership or influence requires more than relationship. Most people have significant relationships with one or more friends, but even so, they might not entrust important business decisions to these friends. To lead a client, a lawyer must have competency in the area of the client's specific legal matter. In some cases, a lawyer may achieve a bespoke or trusted advisor status, so a client expects the lawyer to be competent in every area of the law. It is certainly a good feeling to feel wanted and appreciated in such a comprehensive way; however, the lawyer needs to resist the temptation to be spread too thin. Instead the lawyer should admit the need for an expert in the specific field, because the lawyer's role is to serve the best interest of the client. The alternative is for the lawyer to give advice in an area outside of his or her expertise, risking malpractice. Sometimes a single error can breach a well-established relationship.

Client and industry knowledge. To demonstrate interest in the client, the lawyer must understand facts and circumstances that are relevant to the client. For example, a business client has different needs and concerns than a client on death row. In addition, leaving all the details to others in your firm (assistants and paralegals) so that you constantly need to refer to them when advising a client may not help you become a trusted advisor. Learning key details about a business client might involve visiting the business on your own dime to learn more about what the client does. For other clients, you might need to make other types of contacts to show that your interest in them and their matters goes beyond the amount of your bill.

For the firm leader, it is not only important to be a leader to your own clients but also to strive for the whole firm to be filled with people who desire to excel in lawyer-client relationships. The role of the firm leader in this very important area of leadership includes the following:

1. Assure that the firm hiring process and systems recruit talent that sees relationship as a high priority. To do so, the firm needs more than a platitude in a mission statement; it

needs a culture that elevates the quality of the client relationship above almost all other firm values. During candidate interviews, firm members should focus not only on technical ability and education but, more important, also on a well-balanced personal relations skill.

2. To assure balanced relationship skills, the firm's management committee or practice group leaders should assign teams of professionals to each client. Each team should be well-rounded and balanced both substantively and relationally, with one person being held accountable for assuring that the relationship is maintained and grows.

Questions to Ponder

- Can you identify any lawyers in your firm, or in your community, who seem to relate to their clients as true trusted advisors? What do the lawyers do in their client dealings to establish this kind of relationship?
- Are you guilty of any of the common pitfalls that can injure a close business relationship? What steps can you take in your practice so you can avoid these common pitfalls?
- As a firm leader, what types of things do you focus on when hiring new professionals? Is it possible you should focus more on the relational aspects of a candidate and how he or she would fit into a firm culture that values true client relationships?

Suggested Reading

Dick Wirthlin, *The Greatest Communicator: What Ronald Reagan Taught Me about Politics, Leadership, and Life* (Hoboken, NJ: John Wiley & Sons, 2004).

Jeremie Kubicek, *Leadership Is Dead: How Influence Is Reviving It* (New York: Simon & Schuster, 2011).

LESSON 28 EDUCATION OF FIRM LAWYERS IN THE SKILLS OF LEADING CLIENTS

> *The modern-day firm must be a learning organization. Learning and innovation go hand in hand. The arrogance of success is to think that what you did yesterday will be sufficient for tomorrow. Leaders must set the pace both as teachers and learners.*
>
> —C. William Pollard[67]

A very important job of every law firm leader is guiding lawyers to develop leadership skills. These skills are important for law firm governance and practice management, but every lawyer needs strong leadership skills to represent clients effectively. These skills are generally not taught in law schools. In fact, some law school training works against leadership. For example, the skills of persuasion, though effective when representing clients against an adversary, may make true leadership more difficult. Departing from law school, most associates are thrown into a legal practice armed with legal and persuasion skills but lacking important leadership skills. Law firms, generally made up of people with this same training and education, don't offer much help in this area.

There are exceptions of course, and here are some:

The law firm of Womble Carlyle, based in Winston-Salem, North Carolina, touts a new program it calls Leadership Womble. The goal of the program is described as "developing leaders and maximizing human capital." The firm website (www.wcsr.com/careers/leadership-womble) describes the program as follows:

> This in-house professional development program . . . was developed in cooperation with the Gallup organization. Womble Carlyle already had a

---

67. *The Soul of the Firm*, page 114.

strong existing relationship with Gallup, using the company's Strengths Finder assessment and employee engagement resources management[.] Gallup's "The Demands of Executive Leadership" program has been customized into a law firm leadership program for Womble Carlyle.

The Leadership Womble Program presently draws from the partner levels of the firm and is strictly voluntary. More than 40 people were nominated for the initial class, which first met in September 2010. There is an ongoing nomination list for those within the firm who are interested in participating.

The program requires up to 200 hours of non-billable time over a six-month period. All participants attend three separate, intensive three-day sessions in Washington, D.C. Blackberries are turned off and laptop computers are left in the hotel room, as participants give their undivided attention to the program. The sessions focus on such practical leadership skills as mentoring top talent, building internal and client constituencies, needs of followers, and receiving feedback.

In the interim between class sessions, the participants are divided into three "Leadership Challenge" teams with 4 participants on each team. The "Leadership Challenge"—a project designed to impact issues such as client service, employee engagement and other critical areas for internal improvement—seeks to stretch the resources of our practicing lawyers to support and brainstorm ideas to impact ongoing challenges facing our firm management. The teams discuss their findings with Womble Carlyle's Firm Management Committee during the final Leadership Womble class.

Graduates of Leadership Womble are more aware of their personal leadership style, more receptive to feedback (including input from clients), and better able to motivate others. The program is designed to offer practice professional services leadership in a law firm setting.

At Sidley Austin LLP, a Chicago-based law firm, a special leadership program exists for female attorneys. This firm claims a passion for expanding horizons for women in the firm, for clients of the firm, and for women in the business community. The program is partially social and networking but also brings in big-name female speakers who have become national leaders in both law and business.

Leadership Thought and Application

Many law firms do not have the structure, facilities, or resources to dedicate to such formal leadership programs as the large-firm examples above. Even so, it is critical for law firms to help lawyers develop leadership skills. Consider the following educational ideas for building leadership skills in your firm:

1. **In-house programs.** These programs can be much less formal than those in large firms. Facilitation of the program will likely be the responsibility of firm leadership; however, that is a part of being a leader. Many resources are available to help a leader conduct these programs. Attendees can listen to leadership CDs (for example, the CD that is mailed out to Maximum Impact Club members each month), go through a short workbook together, and discuss application principles. Leadership video series are also available. Another idea is a group leadership program in which each attendee has read the same chapter of a book (perhaps one of the books listed throughout this text) with the group then meeting to discuss the content. Another great idea is to have guest leadership experts make short presentations that challenge firm members with new ideas.

2. **General leadership training events.** These events are generally inexpensive and last a half or full day. Events are now held throughout the country, and some national events are simulcast worldwide. One of my favorite events is Leadercast, founded by John Maxwell, which is held annually in May.

3. **Young lawyer training programs.** One example is the Leadership Academy, which is set up as a partnership

between the North Carolina Bar Association and the Center for Creative Leadership. This program was established to help young lawyers become effective leaders in their work community—the legal profession, a law firm, a legal department, or another workplace. The program recognizes that lawyers are called to be leaders, and until recently lawyers entering the profession have had few opportunities for leadership training. More information about this program can be found at www.ccl.org.

4. **General organized leadership programs.** Colleges and universities (such as Harvard and Georgetown Universities) offer leadership programs, and the Center for Creative Leadership offers all firm leaders a vast number of additional programs (see www.ccl.org). Programs are also offered by many of the law firm consulting companies. Also, the College of Law Practice Management offers a leadership and management program for law firms and lawyers during its annual meeting.

5. **CLE programs.** Several CLE leadership programs are available. For example, ALI CLE offers a program titled Leadership in Practice (see http://www.ali-cle.org/index.cfm?fuseaction=courses.course&course_code=RWSM03).

Finally, the American Bar Association, specifically the Law Practice Management Section, has a huge selection of training resources and materials. Anyone seeking to develop leadership skills should consider becoming an active member of the section.

Questions to Ponder

- What type of leadership development program do you have for yourself? Are you, in some way, being educated to be an effective leader?

- Does your law firm have an organized leadership education plan for its members? Do you believe that such an opportunity should be offered? Do you think it should be encouraged or required?
- Which of the above listed types of programs do you believe would be most effective in your law firm? Why? If you have picked only one method, do you believe that all of your members would properly benefit from such a uniform program? Have you ever tried any group learning sessions in your firm? Would group reading or viewing, followed by discussion, work?

Suggested Reading

C. William Pollard, *The Soul of the Firm* (Grand Rapids, MI: Harper-Collins, 1996).

David H. Maister, *Managing the Professional Services Firm* (New York: Simon & Schuster, 1993).

Chapter 6
DAY-TO-DAY LEADERSHIP

> *Leaders Organize So They Don't Have To Agonize:*
> *Identify and pursue your top priorities.*
> *Seek to practice what will benefit the most people.*
> *Communicate clearly.*
> *See things through the eyes of the outsider.*
> *Order activities simply for the purpose of adding value to others.*
> *Make sure everything is done in an appropriate manner.*
>
> —John C. Maxwell[68]

When focusing on the day-to-day, a leader might be tempted to emphasize management over leadership. However, a leader should look for ways to turn a potentially mundane management issue into a leadership lesson or opportunity. The leadership opportunities discussed throughout this book are not necessarily common occurrences in the everyday business of the practice of law. In contrast, this chapter discusses leadership principles that apply to more common issues that may arise regularly in the life of a law firm:

1. Personnel issues related to the actions or activity of lawyers or staff. The lesson on this topic will address

---

68. *Leadership Promises for Every Day*, page 85.

communication with staff, as well as one of the more difficult issues that comes up in many law firms—bullying.
2. Addressing the very difficult issues in the firm that require consulting the Rules of Professional Conduct. This is a unique consideration for law firms, but one that is quite common.

Suggested Reading

John C. Maxwell, *Leadership Promises for Every Day* (Nashville: Thomas Nelson, 2003).

Barbara Patcher, *The Power of Positive Confrontation: The Skills You Need to Know to Handle Conflicts at Work, at Home, and in Life* (New York: MFJ Books, 2000).

LESSON 29 DEALING WITH PERSONNEL ISSUES

For a conflict to be transformed in an enduring way, all those involved must own the outcome. They must buy in.

—Mark Gerzon[69]

We are a society of structures and hierarchies. Many of these structures and hierarchies have served society well; others are blamed for injustices, challenges, and problems suffered over many centuries. It is human nature for some people to seek to be in charge, while others remain subservient. Many of the achievements that we enjoy today are a result of this type of organizational management structure, which is generally thought of as the system that got us through the Industrial Revolution more than a hundred years ago.

The structure of decision making and control of law firms throughout the country is not uniform, but it is almost without exception a variation of the typical top-down structure. While a typical pyramid structure is beginning to catch on in some larger firms, in almost all smaller and midsize firms owners (shareholders or partners) are in charge of decision making, and all others are below them in the hierarchy. As a result all ultimate control is in the hands of a few. Compensation systems typically do not encourage or reward those who direct (or in effect control) others. Moreover, law firms rarely take the time and effort necessary to assure that those working for the owners are properly trained, compensated, or appreciated.

Given these types of systems and structures, it is understandable that nonpartners express dissatisfaction with their work, especially when it involves receiving and satisfying partners' demands. Law firms may fool themselves with internal team-oriented programs that have been successful in other business organizations. But those

---

69. *Leading through Conflict: How Successful Leaders Transform Differences into Opportunities,* page 58.

programs are a waste of time and effort in a law firm because firm leadership does not hold partners and managers accountable for the way they treat others.

In one law firm, a highly productive paralegal went privately and individually to several members whom she recognized as having authority in the firm: from director to firm administrator to firm billing partner to managing partner. For quite a while she had been overworked and had not received support from others in her practice group. Though she was the most dedicated person in the group, she rarely received appropriate direction and then was belittled by partners when she could not service all of the work she received in the time the partners desired. The real problem was that members of the practice group had not organized as a team. This one paralegal worked for six partners, but no partner, not even the chair of the practice group, was willing to take the time to implement controls and stand up to other partners to reduce the burden on this dedicated assistant. When the paralegal came to those in management, she described the pressures and her feelings. Her main message was that she needed help to get her work done. Although she mentioned her belief that she was undercompensated, this did not seem to be the main point. The work volume and emotional strain was affecting her health, and she did not know how much longer she could deal with the stress. In the overall message of this paralegal was a simple statement, a clue about the root of her dissatisfaction: "It would be nice if someone would simply say thank you from time to time. No one shows any appreciation for the sacrifices I have been willing to make for the firm."

Leadership Thought and Application

Leadership requires thinking outside of the typical box that law firm organizational structures put us in. Many lawyers have struggled to maintain the status quo, a comfortable hierarchy that they believe has served them well, but those who work for demanding and authoritative lawyers need something different. They see change throughout society and are willing to walk away from an intolerable work setting. It is critical for leaders to begin to change their firms so that people who work for partners feel comfortable and appreciated. Although staff do not have law degrees, they need to know that their membership on the team is very important, even though it is different from the role of a lawyer in charge. Making the necessary changes will take time and effort, and most likely it is not possible to make all of the necessary systemic modifications at once. The following considerations can help make your law firm an accepting, uplifting, and supportive organization. The extent of your success will have a direct effect on the number of personnel issues you have and your ability to adequately address them as they arise.

Foster a team environment. It is a leader's task to try to change the mind-set of those in the firm from a hierarchy to a team. Lately the concept of a "team" has gained momentum in law firms, though mostly for substantive work. Many law firms are setting up client teams instead of relying solely on an established practice group system that seems unable to adequately address all of a client's legal needs. This recent trend is based on the belief that one practice group cannot provide organizational clients with comprehensive client service. This same idea applies to those who work for the law firm. Established hierarchies in the firm might have some benefits; however, they are not suited to a changing society that stresses worker empowerment. Leaders must be willing to adapt, but after focusing on their own and others' productivity for so many years, it may be easier to talk about becoming adaptable than to become adaptable. As you lead your lawyers and staff to a team concept, consider the following:

1. **Focus on the firm's mission.** Lawyers tend to focus on themselves: their own hours, their own billing, their own collections. A leader is more likely to be successful in

changing this individual focus of firm members by stressing to them that they focus on how their positive efforts contribute to the firm's overall well-being. However, to convince others to change their focus, the leader must truly desire firm-mindedness.

2. **Overcommunicate the team concept.** At every possible opportunity, remind your team of the firm's team focus and do so sincerely. Firm management and leaders show support of the team focus through their actions. Words alone are not enough. Obviously, this is much easier said than done. Team concepts must, in effect, trickle down from the top.

3. **Institute collaborative systems.** Law firms are generally not collaborative organizations but instead tend to be organizations of small cliques. Practice groups may try to appear collaborative, but compensation systems generally work against cooperation and teamwork. Law firm leaders need to consider how to change firm operations so that collaboration is encouraged. Changes might involve reorganization of work space and relocation, more activities that involve all firm members working on team building (perhaps subtly), or meetings of practice group leaders that focus on internal alliances. The actual means of fostering teamwork in each firm may vary, but teamwork must be a focus.

Address issues of bullying and abuse. Because of traditional governance hierarchies and methods of compensation, law firms are in danger of unnoticed and often unresolved bullying and abuse by firm owners. No one can foster a team environment in a law firm if there is unresolved bullying or abuse. This inappropriate conduct usually arises in the form of a lawyer who oppresses or mistreats a staff member (or several staff members) who supports that lawyer's work. The abuse may take different forms: yelling, ridicule in front of others, inappropriate touching, and other types of improper conduct. Addressing the potential legal liability of such conduct is beyond the scope of this book, but that must always be a consideration when addressing a bully. As a leader of the firm, however, it is imperative that you take action to address bullying as soon as it arises if you truly desire an uplifting and supportive environment. Failure to do so sends the message that bullying is acceptable and that the firm's true values are not necessarily the platitudes set forth in the well-crafted mission and values statements. Depending upon the nature of the improper conduct, a leader may address it privately with the offender and hold the offender accountable. However, depending upon the gravity of the conduct (or perhaps how long the conduct continued unaddressed), a leader might also consider the following general plan of action to address allegations of improper abuse or bullying:

First, bring the conduct to the attention of the full governing body of the firm so it can consider what steps might be taken to investigate the allegations.

Second, after confirmation of the allegations, firm leaders should resolve to conduct an intervention meeting with the bully.

Third, leaders should prepare talking points for the intervention, with specific action items. I recommend the plan include the following:

- Choose an appropriate spokesperson to conduct the meeting, though all management should be present. Because the person being confronted might have a hierarchy view of life, the spokesperson needs to be that person within firm governance who has the greatest respect of the bully.
- Prepare a statement of the reason for the meeting and its purpose or the goal to be gained through it. This will assure that the bully being confronted understands that behavior must be changed.

- A general statement of the offending conduct is sufficient. Avoid the natural tendency to replay specific instances of misconduct, but be clear that you have investigated allegations.
- After stating the charges, express the belief that management values the offending member and that the purpose of the meeting is to plan remediation. The process goal of rehabilitation needs to be made clear. Leaders should also, in no uncertain terms, state with specificity the ultimate consequence of repeated misconduct or failure to complete a required remediation plan.
- Wrap up the meeting with a very specific plan of action. That plan may require treatment or coaching, and it should assign a trusted advisor from management to monitor rehabilitation efforts. Accountability through periodic reporting back to management by the bully and the advisor should be clearly spelled out.

Say thank you. Hierarchy systems do not foster sincere expressions of gratitude by those on the top to those perceived to be underneath. Unless leaders can adequately express gratitude, fostering a team environment that allows law firm staff to feel safe and secure in their membership will likely be very difficult. Leaders may assume that adequate compensation or a raise in pay constitutes expression enough. Generally, however, compensation is what brings people in the door. It may even keep them there in difficult economic times, but it does not instill a sense of togetherness and satisfaction that leads to initiative, innovation, and organizational success.

Expressing gratitude is not just saying the simple phrase *thank you* (which for some is not so simple). Public statements of gratitude, nonmonetary gifts, small periods of time off, and other such expressions can tell team members that they are needed and appreciated.

Questions to Ponder

- Are you a collaborative person? If so, what evidence of collaboration in your law firm can you identify?
- What systems within your firm hinder your ability to instill a sense of teamwork in your firm? What steps can be taken to either replace or marginalize these systems?
- How well do you express gratitude? If you do not express it well, is it because you are so focused and busy? If so, what actions can you take to assure that you will take the time to show your gratitude to others who work for the law firm?

Suggested Reading

Mark Gerzon, *Leading through Conflict: How Successful Leaders Transform Differences into Opportunities* (Boston: Harvard Business School Press, 2006).

Ken Lloyd, *Jerks at Work: How to Deal with People Problems and Problem People* (New York: Barnes & Noble, 2007).

LESSON 30 ETHICS AND THE RULES OF PROFESSIONAL CONDUCT

Sometimes when the numbers look right, the decision is still wrong.

—Kenneth Blanchard and Norman Vincent Peale[70]

Issues related to the ethical conduct of members of your firm are a day-to-day occurrence. Invariably, a firm leader is called upon to make a decision or moderate the discussion on such concerns. Consider these very typical examples of ethics and professionalism issues:

Example 1. Partner A, who is a member of the firm's corporate practice group, has represented a corporate client (Client 1) in the past, on many matters related to the business; however, there has been no representation for years. The corporate minute book is still located on the shelves of the firm, but the client has not made any attempt to respond to inquiries regarding maintenance of the corporate book, and it has not been added to in five years. Partner B is a member of the litigation practice group. A surviving spouse (Client 2) has approached Partner B for representation. The deceased husband was killed in an accident in which a truck owned by Client 1 was being driven during regular business hours by an employee who was impaired due to the use of illegal drugs at the time the accident occurred. Partner B believes the case is very strong against Client 1, which is covered by insurance. Can Partner B take the matter on? Is Client 1 a former client, and is the matter not the same or substantially similar to anything the firm has ever done for Client 1? If it is determined that there is an active conflict of interest, is it one that can be waived? These are all good questions that need to be answered.

---

70. *The Power of Ethical Management*, page 120.

Example 2. Lawyer A represents Client 1 in a litigation matter. Lawyer B is not a member of the firm but has on several occasions attempted to have Lawyer A disqualified from matters based on ethics grounds that the firm believes have no merit. It is believed that Lawyer B attempts to use the Rules of Professional Conduct to make disqualification motions as a tactical ploy. A pattern of abuse can be found. Should, or must, this seeming abuse of the Rules be reported to the state bar? Does the duty to report misconduct apply? Might a complaint against Lawyer B seem the same as Lawyer A's previous complaints against Lawyer B?

Example 3. Lawyer A represents Client 1 in a matter where the firm will be receiving $3 million into trust, a sum that must be divided and paid out to several parties, one of which is the firm, which will also be receiving substantial attorney fees. It is very close to the end of the year (last day is tomorrow), and Lawyer A would really like to have the fee collected before year-end because of the potential for a substantial annual bonus. Payment is received in the form of an out-of-state personal check. This is the first matter in which the firm has represented Client 1. Should the firm deposit and disburse the funds represented by the check? If the firm's banking institution is willing to provide the firm with provisional credit, should the firm rely on this credit and disburse funds prior to actual collection?

All of these fact scenarios cry out for a leader who not only knows the Rules of Professional Conduct, but whose advice is respected enough to be followed and who has an established firm ethics procedure to rely on when making a determination.

Leadership Thought and Application

Firm leaders, especially in larger law firms, are often tempted to delegate the authority and responsibility for rules compliance to another trusted advisor in the firm. This common practice may be the right answer for your firm. In smaller law firms there may be a temptation to allow every lawyer to make his or her own decisions on ethics issues that arise and specifically to allow individual lawyers to work out their disagreements without the oversight of a third-party leader unless the disagreement cannot be resolved. These situations often do not present a level playing field; for example, an associate and a partner have a difference in bargaining power, and the partner is more likely to prevail. One justification is that the partner is much more learned in ethics and professionalism and can use the issue as a learning tool for the associate. However, the number of years that a lawyer has been in practice is not always an indicator of greater ethics understanding or behavior.

Every leader tempted to delegate responsibility for ethics compliance needs to be aware of Rule 5.1 of the ABA Model Rules of Professional Conduct (which has been adopted as a rule in most states in one form or another):

Law Firms and Associations
Rule 5.1 Responsibilities of Partners, Managers, and Supervisory Lawyers

(a) A partner in a law firm, and a lawyer who individually or together with other lawyers possesses comparable managerial authority in a law firm, shall make reasonable efforts to ensure that the firm has in effect measures giving reasonable assurance that all lawyers in the firm conform to the Rules of Professional Conduct.

(b) A lawyer having direct supervisory authority over another lawyer shall make reasonable efforts to ensure that the other lawyer conforms to the Rules of Professional Conduct.

(c) A lawyer shall be responsible for another lawyer's violation of the Rules of Professional Conduct if:

> (1) the lawyer orders or, with knowledge of the specific conduct, ratifies the conduct involved; or
>
> (2) the lawyer is a partner or has comparable managerial authority in the law firm in which the other lawyer practices, or has direct supervi-

sory authority over the other lawyer, and knows of the conduct at a time when its consequences can be avoided or mitigated but fails to take reasonable remedial action.

This one rule is most likely the single scariest rule or regulation for a managing partner or any other partner with supervisory authority in a law firm. When it comes to law firm leadership, Rule 5.1 essentially says that a law firm leader really is his or her brother's keeper. If a lawyer with leadership authority decides to delegate responsibility for ethics compliance, it is done at his or her own risk. This does not mean that authority and responsibility should not be delegated, but it does mean that the leader should have sufficient oversight to assure ethics compliance. A leader might consider a few basic principles regarding ethics and rules compliance:

1. **The Model Rules of Professional Conduct are a floor and not a ceiling.** Ethics dilemmas in a law firm often begin with the phrase "Can I...?" Certainly these questions must be answered from the outset. However, the next question to consider is "Should we ... ?" The Rules of Professional Conduct set forth a minimal level of consideration and compliance that must be adhered to, but they do not set forth the maximum standard of professionalism a firm might consider. Notice that the second question is *Should we* ... ?

    Ethics compliance in a law firm is not an individual proposition, but a team proposition, and not just because Rule 5.1 puts the burden on leaders to assure compliance. It is a team proposition because every decision to be made needs to be considered in light of how it might affect the entire law firm. The answer to "Should we . . . ?" is not merely decided by considering whether an action will result in a state bar complaint against anyone. Quite simply, a leader must consider whether it is the right thing to do. In addition, business decisions may be needed. For instance, in a conflict-of-interest situation, should the matter be taken even if the opposing party is a former client who has had no contact with the firm in several years? Even if firm members consider the party as a former client, is that how that client would consider himself or herself? Would the client instead believe he or she had purchased some degree of loyalty from the firm for the past work? All these issues need to be considered, and the written rules simply do not provide complete guidance on what is right and what is wrong. It is the job of a good leader to assure that these questions are always being asked and answered in a way that is fair to the individual lawyers, to the firm and its reputation, and to the clients (current or future) or potential clients considering their reasonable expectations.

2. **Resist the urge to say yes, when the correct answer is no.** Even though Rule 5.1 has been adopted in most of the states, leaders have a tendency to give in and say yes to conduct that is borderline, even when the correct answer is no. In one firm, a group of four lawyers sat around for over two hours discussing whether the firm's litigation practice group should take a certain matter. The matter could have been quite profitable. Finally the firm leader said, "Look, we have been sitting here two hours now and we are not any closer to resolution of this matter. The fact that we cannot decide on the ethics issue here should give us some basis upon which to say that the answer is no. If we cannot collectively agree, then the answer really should be no." The leader's words are the moral of the story and perhaps good advice for any law firm leader. Many different considerations may entice the team and perhaps its leader to say yes to a new client matter. In many cases the pressure may be financial, but in other cases it may be other firm priorities. However, no consideration is higher than the ethical reputation of the firm, and leaders need to resist the temptation to satisfy an immediate need by compromising their bedrock principles.

3. Take the lead in ethics training and leadership. Generally law firms do not go out of their way to provide ethics and professional responsibility training, perhaps because firm leaders assume that lawyers understand ethics because they have passed the multistate ethics exam. In addition, many state bars now require CLE in the area of ethics and professional responsibility, either as a part of the overall annual CLE requirement or as a stand-alone component every several years. Leaders need to recognize that these regulatory requirements represent a floor for keeping one's license. For that reason, firm leaders should regularly encourage ethics discussion among the lawyers. As a group, team members need to understand the firm's ethics and professional responsibility standards and goals as described in the mission and vision statements. Discussions may be informal; for example, at regularly scheduled firm meetings, such as weekly or monthly breakfast meetings of the entire firm or regular meetings of practice groups in larger firms. In states that require ethics CLE, hourly requirements are generally short. Because online CLE is now available in most states, a regular meeting might include an ethics video followed by time for firm members to collectively discuss the video's content and ethical situations. It is the leader's job to find ways to assure that all lawyers in the firm understand the firm's (1) priority for ethical behavior in all its members, (2) desire to far exceed the baseline of ethical and professional conduct established in the Rules, (3) intolerance for violations of established ethical and professionalism standards, and (4) procedures to assure compliance with the standards.

Questions to Ponder

- Are you committed to the principle that there is no right way to do something that is wrong?
- What are some firm values that may tempt you to make decisions that may not fully comply with the Rules or the firm's professional conduct standards?
- Does your firm have established procedures for addressing ethics and rules compliance issues that may arise? Are they adequate? If adequate, are there areas that need to be updated or revised? Do all firm members know the terms of the procedures?
- Are unlicensed staff aware of ethics and professional rules and the established procedures related to compliance? Is there proper oversight regarding the conduct of nonlawyer staff?

Suggested Reading

Kenneth Blanchard and Norman Vincent Peale, *The Power of Ethical Management* (New York: William Morrow & Company, 1988).

Michael Novak, *Business as a Calling: Work and the Examined Life* (New York: Simon & Schuster, 1996).

Chapter 7
STRATEGY AND PLANNING— CASTING VISION

It's kind of fun to do the impossible.

—Walt Disney[71]

Vision is a clear mental picture of what could be, fueled by the conviction that it should be. Vision is a preferred future. A destination. Vision always stands in contrast to the world the way it is. Vision demands change. It implies movement. . . . Vision requires visionaries, people who have allowed their minds and hearts to wander outside the artificial boundaries imposed by the world as it is. A vision requires an individual who has the courage to act out an idea.

—Andy Stanley[72]

Every organization, law firms included, must have both a mission and a vision for the future. Simply put, a mission is what the firm is all about: its purpose, why it exists, and what it wants to accomplish. Its vision is where it wants to go and what it wants to be in the future. So many law firm mission statements look the same and seem to lack specific and individual purpose. They tend to be filled

---

71. *Animated Architecture* (1982) by Derek Walker, page 10.
72. *Visioneering: God's Blueprint for Developing and Maintaining Vision*, page 18.

with platitudes about excellent service and high ethical standards. Perhaps these aims should be included; however, every firm-specific mission statement also needs to be specifically worded to fit the individual law firm, incorporating something significant about what distinguishes its culture from that of other firms.

Although most firms have a stated mission and purpose, the articles on the popular website Above the Law (http://abovethelaw.com) suggest that most law firm associates believe that practicing law is all about money. Few articles on that website relate associate satisfaction to anything other than salary, benefits, and job satisfaction, indicating that most law firms do not highlight purpose and mission as a major focus with their firm members. Perhaps some owners focus on purpose and vision; however, casting vision throughout the firm does not seem to be a primary objective of most law firm managers. Nevertheless, it should be. Strategy and planning must be firm wide and must incorporate employees from all parts of the firm. A well-rounded planning process is a basic principle that applies to all business organizations, and law firms are not exempt from it. Without a well-rounded planning process, the results will likely be flawed and lead to failure. This chapter begins with a lesson that examines the lawyer leader's role in the strategic planning process. Certain duties can be delegated, and authority and involvement should be shared, but leaders need to supervise the process itself, and hold others accountable for the tasks they have agreed to undertake. The next lesson considers the possibility that the planning process itself can be a leadership opportunity. This lesson asks the question whether every law firm should spend time on the strategic planning process, and if so, what the leaders of the process might focus on developing a strategic plan, and a few general concerns or potential pitfalls to avoid.

Suggested Reading

Andy Stanley, *Visioneering: God's Blueprint for Developing and Maintaining Vision* (Colorado Springs: Random House, 1999).

Andy Stanley, *Making Vision Stick* (Grand Rapids, MI: Zondervan, 2007).

LESSON 31 THE ROLE OF THE FIRM LEADER IN STRATEGIC PLANNING

If an organization's leaders want their people to believe that a new strategy is being followed, they must establish credibility by proving that they are prepared to change themselves: how they act, measure, and reward.

—David H. Maister[73]

Strategic planning is not an easy process for most law firms. A failure in the process is usually due to a failure of firm leadership. Unfortunately, as previously mentioned, law firm leadership is much different from leadership in other organizations due to the typical experiences, education, and practice settings of firm stakeholders. It is both my observation and experience that all of the typical rules and processes of strategic planning, such as establishing a mission; casting a vision; agreeing upon values; setting goals, objectives, strategies, tactics, and accountability; and regular follow-up and evaluation, apply to law firm strategic planning. In addition, however, law firm decision makers are mostly owners and feel that they should not only have an equal say in all matters of importance but also have veto power over anything that might affect their individual lives. Members often sit around a table and argue the merits of various paths for the future as if they are arguing a case in court. Partner owners generally have become accustomed to making decisions by sitting in a room and discussing how things should be. They believe that everyone's opinion is equal on every issue and that the loudest or most persuasive speaker will rule the day. Instead of leading a process to determine the future direction of the firm as an entity, the leader usually has to manage disagreements about how the firm should use scarce resources in the near future.

---

73. *Strategy and the Fat Smoker: Doing What's Obvious but Not Easy*, page 11.

Some firms have strategic planning retreats with interesting guest speakers over pleasurable weekends. General observations of professional trends are discussed, usually without meaningful application to the firm. One might argue that these superficial retreats are positive because they foster camaraderie, but if they do not include some meaningful strategic planning, their usefulness is questionable. In these cases, any unspoken issues generally remain pent-up inside members. At some point, however, the issues are likely to become public during a verbal confrontation or when one or more members escape the firm for perceived greener pastures.

In other cases, leaders create a legitimate and productive process, but the meeting degrades into bitter and divisive confrontations, where elephants in the room are revealed in unhelpful ways. The strategic planning a leader had intended is pushed aside to settle personality disputes and grievances about mundane and current problems. Leaders may walk away wondering if they should never have started the process in the first place.

Leadership Thought and Application

Leadership's primary role in strategic planning is to cast vision and to make it stick among firm stakeholders. As is the case in most areas of leadership, casting vision is much easier said than done. In fact, what does *casting vision* really mean in a law firm?

Specifically, it means that a leader takes responsibility for wording, understanding, explaining, and personally exemplifying the mission, vision, and values of the law firm. The responsibility to exemplify the firm's mission, vision, and values extends to all levels in the firm. To cast vision in a law firm, a leader should consider the following:

1. **Statement of mission and vision.** Strategic planning begins with mission and vision. Without defining both of these, you cannot plan any type of strategy. The leader of a

law firm must be a well-rounded student of the firm—the entire firm, not just one group—and its market. He or she must take all of that knowledge and understanding and define the firm's purpose and identify where the firm is headed. It is crucial that mission and vision be stated as succinctly as possible in a way that can be explained and remembered easily. A leader can use a well-stated mission and vision to get discussions, meetings, and confrontations back on track if they have taken a personal, nonstrategic route that does not enhance the firm.

2. **Justify the plan.** It is not sufficient for a leader to only be able to explain the mission and vision of the firm clearly and concisely. He or she must also be able to logically explain why the plan is a priority, and that requires a convincing argument about how the plan reflects the shared values of the firm. Of course, the mission and vision must be consistent with the values that all members agree on. A very important part of the leader's role is to tie together these three crucial parts (mission, vision and values) of the planning process. However, because lawyers like to debate almost every point, the leader must be able to make a convincing argument. If so, it will be easier for the leader to bring the team back together in times of trouble or controversy. If the leader fails to make a clear and argument tying the mission and vision to the members' shared values, the jury (stakeholders) will rule against him or her.

3. **Reinforce the vision.** As often as possible, the leader needs to restate the agreed-upon vision. And as often as possible, management's actions need to be tied to the firm's mission and vision. If leaders simply say that they buy into the strategic plan and do not live the plan personally they will not be able to reinforce it. Whenever leaders find that their actions are not consistent with the values, mission, or vision, it is

very important that they own up to the mistake, modify conduct, and apologize to any person or group that have been affected. A mistake in personal leadership without immediate acknowledgment and correction will certainly result in lost trust and failure. On the other hand, followers do not expect a leader to be perfect. If they observe that the leader's commitment to the firm is so great that he or she admits a mistake and corrects future conduct, they will follow and be more open to correction when they make mistakes.

More generally, a leader's role in the strategic planning process is to lead the organization and its members in preparation for for the future. The process should accomplish the following:

1. **Protect the organization and its people.** Protection allows followers to achieve the organizational purpose and their individual purpose. Of course, followers must understand these purposes, and it is the job of the leader to facilitate education and understanding.

2. **Preserve the identity of the people.** The leader needs to conduct the process in such a way that members of the organization feel like they belong to and are a part of the organization.

3. **Provides for the members of the firm and its clients.** The process needs to consider what the organization will provide to meet the changing needs of firm members and clients in the short term as well as the long term. The leader needs the flexibility to make changes in how and what the organization will provide.

The bottom line is that the strategic planning process must constantly remind members not of their independence, but of their dependence on each other and the organization to achieve a common individual goals and those consistent individual goals of each member and client.

Questions to Ponder

- Who is involved in the strategic planning process of your firm? Who among that group is responsible for casting vision and making it stick with members of the firm? Are there any parts of the strategic planning process that leaders need to change?
- As a leader, how often do you reinforce the strategic plan to members of the firm? Do you find that you do not have time to do so? Do you find that day-to-day problems keep you from this strategic role? What types of systems can you put in place in your own life to remind you of your strategic role?
- Do you believe that all of the members of your law firm (1) think they are part of a greater organizational purpose, (2) have an organizational identity, and (3) are provided for by the firm?

Suggested Reading

David H. Maister, *Strategy and the Fat Smoker: Doing What's Obvious but Not Easy* (Boston: Spangle Press, 2008).

John J. Michalik, *The Extraordinary Managing Partner: Reaching the Pinnacle of Law Firm Management* (Lincolnshire, IL: Association of Legal Administrators, 2011).

LESSON 32 THE PROCESS OF STRATEGIC PLANNING—IS IT FOR EVERYONE?

> *The simple fact is that when a firm makes it all about money, little else matters. . . . The lesson to be learned has . . . to do with tying people together with a shared vision, purpose and culture. . . . Money can be an important part of the vision, but it has to be the result of achievement, not the purpose for being. In law firms money can be good—greed can't.*
>
> —H. Edward Wesemann[74]

I can argue that strategic planning is a valuable process for any law firm, and I can also argue that for some firms the process can be a colossal waste of time.

Consider this scenario. A firm leader desires to begin the strategic planning process, believing that the eventual outcome can only help the firm's future. He or she involves the firm's management committee in a long ordeal of executive planning for the process. Firm members receive notice of the date and time for the meetings and an explanation that, for the most part, members of management will lead the stages in the process. Much time is spent planning firm member surveys, and much effort goes into planning meetings to discuss firm strengths, weaknesses, opportunities, and threats. But very little time is spent determining whether members are willing to commit to the process or the collective decisions it involves. In initial meetings firm owners pay lip service to the process; however, outside the meetings, stakeholders whisper in the hallway about lost billable time. The outward consensus to the process and results sugar coats most members' underlying views. They agree to endure planning and agree with the positive effects it may have on others,

---

74. *The First Great Myth of Legal Management Is That It Exists: Tough Issues for Law Firm Managing Partners and Administrators,* pages 88–89.

but they do not want it to affect them personally (or in any way that requires them to make changes).

Once all of the meetings are done, due to the details of day-to-day practice, the management committee takes months to get a final strategic planning report to the firm members, who by that time have lost almost all interest. The plan is debated and revised by firm members, who agree to the principles it contains. However, as they debate, they vote to make revisions, deleting almost all of the accountability and evaluation processes in it. The plan is approved and published in a nice bound notebook that is put on each member's bookshelf, never to be opened or referred to again.

Leadership Thought and Application

Simply put, strategic planning is a process by which law firm stakeholders (not only owners but all members of the firm, from partner to legal assistant), whatever the size of the firm, collectively define the following:

1. Who are we?
2. Who's out there?
3. Whom do we want to be?
4. How do we get there?
5. How are we going to execute our plan to get there?

Before embarking on the process, firm owners must be committed to it. Strategic planning is not just an intellectual exercise. It is meant to be a very valuable tool to assure the firm's future success. Unfortunately, without sufficient commitment of members to the demands of implementing the plan, the result may be a well-written and attractive document. In some cases, firm leaders may express a solid commitment to strategic planning, but they seem more committed to drafting a fancy wish list of things they know will never be done. Commitment to writing a plan but not to the whole process is simply a colossal waste of time and effort. However, having a mission and strategic vision for the future is in the best interest of any law firm, considering how dramatically the legal profession has changed and will likely continue to change.

Some firm leaders might read the preceding paragraph and conclude that strategic planning is not for them. They may feel that it is a waste of time and that the status quo is just fine. Many different reasons can lead to this conclusion. Some of these leaders are willing to accept the risks of failing to plan, and others are satisfied with informal, noncomprehensive (though inadequate) planning, such as buying insurance, that most businesses can do without much expenditure of time. For all of those failing to plan, the rate and extent of change will simply be a gamble—risks that they must be willing to take.

A problem is that many law firm leaders will not admit that they do not want to employ a strategic planning process. Instead they usually make a verbal commitment to a process that turns out to be a waste of time for them and for their firms. Don't try to fake the process or your commitment to it. A strategic planning process without follow-through only harms the morale of members who believed that their leader was actually interested. If you don't have a sufficient and genuine commitment, you won't fool anyone. A written plan that sits on the shelf with action items unfulfilled will simply be a reminder that leadership has failed.

Process questions. Consider your response and the response of all firm stakeholders to these important process questions. If the responses show that a firm-wide commitment is lacking, strategic planning might not be the best expenditure of time for your firm.

1. **Are we willing to change the systems within our organization that hinder strategic planning?**

    If you truly desire successful strategic planning, you must make the process a priority. Certainly billable work is important, and the money must come in to pay the bills. However, strategic planning is about the long-term viability of the firm. Without a commitment to making it a priority (which might include incentivizing follow-through), going through the steps is a waste of your time. Through the process you will also probably find that nonbillable efforts that help the firm achieve future success need to be encouraged and recognized. Will the firm also be willing to change in this area?

2. **Are all firm members truly committed to the process and not just paying lip service to it?**

   Leaders must figure out if there are firm members who verbally agree to the process, but are not truly interested in it, because they will be a hindrance. Especially in smaller firms, it does not take much negative energy to trip up the time-consuming process of strategic planning. Firm leadership must neutralize negativity or not engage in the process. The answer to this question is often quite difficult to deal with, but unless you are willing to make the hard decisions necessary to neutralize dissent (which in some cases requires the dissenters' separation), there is no reason to waste time.

3. **Is firm leadership willing to say no to perceived business opportunities that are not in line with the plan?**

   The strategic planning process for any law firm, regardless of size, examines the firm's desired practice areas and attempts to align them with the future of the profession. Once a plan is agreed to, some of the firm's current practice areas may not be identified as areas to be continue pursuing. A firm hungry for work tends to say yes to anything and everything that comes through the door, but that may not be in its long-term interest. For instance, a law firm with a small but profitable insurance defense practice was concerned that it could not build a personal injury or products liability practice. As part of the strategic planning process, the firm investigated why it did not get personal injury and products liability referrals. It discovered that conflicts of interest and a perception caused by the insurance defense practice seemed to be limiting its expansion into these areas. Because the strategic planning process had identified the goal of building the personal injury and products liability practice, the firm would need to turn away all insurance defense work. At first, it was tough going as the firm turned away what it considered bread-and-butter before the other areas had been built into thriving practices. However, the firm remained committed to the process and turned away insurance defense matters. Eventually the legal community's perception changed, and the firm was able to build a substantial and thriving practice in personal injury and products liability.

4. **Will your firm members be able to work as a team throughout the process?**

   For small and solo firms, this question is key, and the answer must be yes. The smaller a law firm, the more likely the members are autonomous (also common in larger law firms). They are also likely to feel entitled to autonomy and expect others to respect their autonomy. Simply put, strategic planning in any organization of more than one person is a team process and requires team commitment and follow-through on the results. Even for a law firm with one lawyer and one support staff member, the process needs to be a team effort. Autonomy does not work well in the collaborative environment that strategic planning requires. Unless there is team thinking and firm-mindedness, consider saving the time and effort needed for strategic planning.

To answer these questions in a positive manner for the long-term success of the firm, the role of the leader in the process will have to be taken seriously (see Lesson 31 for a discussion of the leader's role). As leaders of the strategic planning process think about how to move forward, they should also consider a few additional factors:

1. **Don't get too hung up on the form your planning takes, just make sure it covers all of the major factors.** Too much time and effort is often spent on the formalities of strategic planning. Further, the actual term *strategic planning* can evoke negative feelings in many who believe it is a waste of time. Leaders need to use different names for the process and look for new and innovative ways to excite firm members about change. Instead of calling the process strategic planning, consider using an event, crisis, or common theme as a reason to plan the firm's future. For example, conduct an economic downturn summit, a marketing conference, or a succession-planning meeting.

2. **Don't be fooled into believing that your firm has special circumstances so strategic planning, which may be fine for others, does not apply.** This misconception is very common in smaller firms in smaller cities or towns. People must realize that the economy is global now. They need to be convinced that the firm can simply no longer hide its organizational head in the sand. The leader of the process must be prepared to address how changes that seem global will affect the firm in the short term and well into the future.

3. **Don't focus too much internally.** The primary focus of strategic planning should be the firm's place in the legal market, both geographically and by practice area. Some internal focus is necessary because operations have a direct impact on competitive effectiveness. However, too much internal focus can direct attention away from strategy and place it on day-to-day management issues.

4. **Strategic planning needs to be about making the pie larger.** If the main purpose of a retreat or so-called

planning session is how to divide up the income, the meeting is not strategic planning. Compensation is not a focus of the strategic planning process. Certainly one of the key jobs of a good leader and management team is helping the law firm establish a fair compensation system, one that provides appropriate incentives. Although the compensation plan should be consistent with the strategic plan, the process of establishing a compensation plan should be separate from the strategic planning process.

5. **Bespoke is the exception rather than the rule.** The practice of law is getting more and more competitive, as traditional legal services are being performed by people other than lawyers. Lawyers have a tendency to see themselves and the services they provide as special (see Lesson 27 for a discussion of a bespoke, or trusted and engaged, advisor). Leaders need to assure that the process of planning encourages stakeholders to differentiate their services from those provided by others, and therefore help firm members understand that sooner or later most legal services will be seen as commodities.

6. **Include stakeholder naysayers, but do not let them hijack the process.** It is hugely important that all firm members understand that the process has been established to allow all stakeholders some input into how the firm's future will be planned. At the same time, every organization has certain people who will, if allowed, become obstacles to success. Leaders need to identify these people and assure they are treated fairly in the process, but should not allow them to become a hindrance.

7. **Tactic implementation should not await a final written plan.** Change is occurring so fast that before the ink is dry on the final document, some tactics in a traditional strategic plan will no longer be relevant. As the process starts, identify action

items that are not controversial and create strategies and tactics that all members of the firm will agree on. A leader should quickly bring these items forward for consideration, get buy-in, and move ahead as soon as possible.

Questions to Ponder

- As a leader, how do you answer process questions 1–4? How would other firm stakeholders answer the questions? Based on these answers, are you wasting time by planning?
- Have you personally been active in your firm's strategic planning process? Have you hired consultants to help with the process? What has been your experience with the process? What changes based on past experience should be made to future planning efforts?
- Is your planning process more internally focused? If so, what types of issues are the biggest internal concerns? As a leader, what steps can you take to move those internally focused issues out of your strategic planning process?

Suggested Reading

H. Edward Wesemann, *The First Great Myth of Legal Management Is That It Exists: Tough Issues for Law Firm Managing Partners and Administrators* (Bloomington, IN: Authorhouse, 2004).

David H. Maister, *Strategy and the Fat Smoker: Doing What's Obvious but Not Easy* (Boston: Spangle Press, 2008).

Seth Godin, *Poke the Box* (Do You Zoom, 2011).

Chapter 8
LEADING THROUGH A CRISIS

LESSON 33 STRENGTH AND COURAGE IN TIMES OF TROUBLE

> *Thematic Goal: a single qualitative focus that is shared by the entire leadership team—and ultimately, by the entire organization—and that applies for only a specified period of time.*
>
> —Patrick Lencioni[75]

A law firm crisis can take many different forms. There are so many different kinds of difficulties that I originally considered dividing this topic into four or five separate lessons, each addressing a different kind of crisis. Instead, I chose one lesson because, no matter what kind of crisis arises, leaders have similar opportunities and threats to deal with, and the leader's reaction—in both thought and deed—determines the consequences that eventually result. In some cases, a difficult situation can blow up into a crisis. A dictionary

---

75. *Silos, Politics and Turf Wars: A Leadership Fable about Destroying the Barriers That Turn Colleagues into Competitors,* page 178.

definition of *crisis* is "a crucial time or decisive moment." Law firm leaders need to realize that members of the firm can perceive a simple but difficult situation as a crisis. Certainly every leader of a law firm will encounter difficult situations that he or she must handle. Sometimes a situation may even amount to a crisis that needs immediate action. Consider the following situations that I relate from experience:

1. **A personal crisis of an individual of the firm.** Difficult times in an individual's life—whether work related or personal—invariably affect work and productivity. A member may have a spouse or child in the hospital, or perhaps it is the lawyer who has a health issue. A lawyer might be dealing with an emotional or substance abuse issue. Professional conduct issues in need of remediation can cause difficulty for a member.

2. **Partner departure.** Perhaps a whole practice group is raided by another law firm, and all its members leave to go to work in what seem like greener pastures. Maybe the firm's highest biller leaves with very little notice, taking staff, client files, and a significant book of business.

3. **Loss of a valuable firm administrator.** It is problem enough for a firm leader to deal with partner-level and strategic issues. Generally a managing partner leaves administrative tasks to a firm administrator. Losing a firm administrator can feel like a crisis to a managing partner. I know because I have lost two firm administrators to larger firms in the last twelve years. The loss might not seem so large to other firm members, but it is for the managing partner who now has to manage the day-to-day administrative tasks until a replacement can be found.

4. **Technology issues.** Although technology crises can come in many different forms, the most obvious crises today are an e-mail system that stops working properly for an extended

period of time and loss of access to an electronic document management system.

5. **Loss of a valuable trained associate.** The short-term problem of losing an associate does not seem so critical, but departure of a trusted associate who has built up a substantial practice can create a crisis, even without considering the substantial amount of time and money spent on training over the years.

6. **Death.** Unfortunately my firm has gone through this crisis too frequently in recent years. We lost a former managing partner and watched a staff member wither away from cancer. Events such as these can certainly be a crisis for the firm. Although lawyers and their staff are quite good at putting up a hard and rugged front to the other side in a legal matter, they often do not handle crisis in their midst very well. I have also discovered that some lawyers may stay focused on their work as a way of avoiding grief, and appear to others as insensitive.

7. **Disaster.** Certainly natural disasters such as hurricanes, floods, or fire can cause a crisis, as can disasters caused by people, such as those related to crime.

And the list goes on.

Leadership Thought and Application

Leadership in times of crisis is evident in a leader's attitude and the action he or she is willing to take.

Attitude—strong and courageous leadership in times of trouble. People need a good leader in tough times and especially in times of crisis. They need someone who is strong and courageous, although the way leaders express strength and humility may be surprising:

- First, and seemingly counterintuitive, a leader must be humble toward followers, including everyone else in the law firm and clients. Generally speaking, in my experience, *humble* is not a word that is often used to describe lawyers. Realizing who you are and understanding the limits of your strengths and the power of your weaknesses in a difficult situation brings humility. A humble leader understands the need for and dependency on other members of the firm. A leader must recognize that there is no place for pride in the time of trouble.
- Second, a strong and courageous leader must stick to certain principles, such as the firm mission, vision, and values, even when moving away from these principles might seem expedient. For example, during the recent recession, downsizing, or reducing head count (a very impersonal way to describe putting valued employees out of work), seemed expedient. However, keeping staff was more difficult and required strength and courage, even though in the short term it seemed financially costly. In tough times, a strong and courageous leader will stay focused on the mission and convey that focus to others. It's not about being a hero, but it is about staying the course on the everyday work and life of the firm.
- Third, a strong and courageous leader understands that not every crisis is all bad, even if it is painful in the short term. A crisis may itself be a blessing because it helps shape a leader's character. A crisis may cause pain, but it may turn out to be a positive experience that leads to future success.

Being a strong and courageous leader in times of trouble or crisis will help create the following:

1. **A sense of security in followers.** Without this kind of leadership, followers tend to flee. They desire a safe place of employment and will look for another law firm if they do not feel secure. Strong leadership, however, encourages followers to move toward and support each other.

2. **The followers' belief that they need their leader.** Followers will stick with their leader because they will feel comfortable staying in their jobs, and they will also feel empowered as they see the leader's strength.

Action—firm, fair, and focused on the future. In times of crisis, the actions of a leader are very important. With a plan, leaders are more able to act calmly and keep their focus on the future.

1. **Have a plan for difficult times.** Obviously a law firm cannot have a plan for every possible crisis, but certain types of crises are so common they merit advanced planning. These crises include natural disasters (weather related, earthquake, etc.), departure of significant lawyers (such as a whole practice group), technology failures, or certain types of personal issues. These plans should also include generic procedures and policies that would apply to almost any difficulty. A leader should openly discuss these policies and procedures so that members understand the importance of and know how to maintain solidarity. The greater the member buy-in to the processes and procedures to be employed in times of trouble, the more likely the team will stay together and the leader will be able to lead when difficult times arise.

2. **Be the calm in the storm.** In any crisis people tend to react emotionally before they have had time to think of an appropriate response. A leader, however, must be level-headed, thoughtful, and considerate. In addition, he or she needs to make sure others do not react without considering possible repercussions. A leader needs self-control and must maintain composure. To temper the conduct of others requires leadership, or influence. Leaders need to realize that a crisis is an opportunity to solidify the trust and respect of followers, but it is also a time of great risk. Overcommunicating, staying calm and collected, and responding in a

logical and well-thought-out manner goes a long way to solidify respect from followers. And with that respect, a leader is more able to lead.

3. **Be fair but firm minded** Many crisis situations involve another party, a person or group that has wronged the firm or is causing it distress. Human nature seeks retribution or punishment, but a leader should resist this temptation. All eyes—not only those on the other side—are watching to see how the leader will respond. Firm members want to see that their leaders are fair, in part because they could imagine themselves in a similar situation. Further, members want leadership to act in the firm's best interest because they each have a stake in the long-term viability of the organization.

4. **Make lemonade out of lemons** Recently a politician made a comment that an organization should not miss the opportunity in any crisis. Every law firm crisis should be seen as an opportunity for team achievement and success. A crisis is an opportunity to break down the walls that divide a firm, practice group, or other team of professionals. A leader should consider whether a crisis is also an opportunity to break up silos (formal or informal structures) within the firm that might be causing division. When a crisis occurs, a leader should bring the whole organization together and consider whether all the members can circle around a common short-term goal or mission. For instance, if a practice group departs for perceived greener pastures, it is likely that one or more of the other practice groups or factions have also congregated into silos. In this type of a crisis, a firm will likely experience the threats of lost revenues, lost clients, and fewer lawyers to bill the hours necessary to cover fixed overhead expenses. It is a perfect opportunity for a leader to call the whole firm together and rally the troops

around establishing a plan to sustain the firm through the difficult process of rebuilding.

Questions to Ponder

- When your law firm is hit with a crisis, how do you pull people together? Do you see a crisis as an opportunity or a threat?
- What is the hardest part of leading in a time of crisis?
- Does your firm, or the group within the firm that you lead, have a plan for difficult times? If so, is it comprehensive? Are there some difficulties that you are neither specifically nor generally ready for? What needs to be done to better prepare?

Suggested Reading

Patrick Lencioni, *Politics and Turf Wars: A Leadership Fable about Destroying the Barriers That Turn Colleagues into Competitors* (San Francisco: Jossey-Bass, 2006).

Allen R. Cohen, *Influence without Authority* (New York: John Wiley & Sons, 1989).

Chapter 9
SUCCESSION PLANNING: LEAVING A LEGACY FOR THE NEXT GENERATION

You, Cambyses, must never forget that the empire isn't guarded by magic. If you succeed, it will only be through the strength of your faithful friends. Think of how well I was served by such noble souls as Mandarus and Kryzantos. You must never imagine that such loyal hearts spring up like grass in the field. No, every leader must actively raise up his followers, and you must win their hearts by the kindness that springs from love.

—Xenophon[76]

It is the responsibility of every leader to finish well. For a law firm leader, finishing well is more than simply leaving the entity that you lead—the law firm, a practice group, or a committee—in the same condition as when you first took the reins. For the true firm leader, retirement or stepping down is also more than leaving in such a way that your retirement fund does not break the firm's bank. It is about leaving the next generation with a mission and a vision for the future. It is critical for every law firm to have a strategic plan, and for the plan to be effective it must address succession. Further,

---

76. *Xenophon's* Cyrus the Great: *The Arts of Leadership and War*, ed. Larry Hedrick, page 291.

succession planning should always consider at least the following three areas of concern:

1. Succession or growth of the firm's substantive practice;
2. Succession of each individual's practice from an older generation to a younger generation, including training of and work flow to the younger generation; and
3. Succession of firm management and leadership into and out of positions of authority and service.

Suggested Reading

Larry Hedrick, ed., *Xenophon's* Cyrus the Great: *The Arts of Leadership and War* (New York: St. Martin's Press, 2006).

Max Depree, *Leading without Power: Finding Hope in Serving Community* (San Francisco: Jossey-Bass, 1997).

LESSON 34 PLANNING TO PLAN[77]

The Law of Legacy: A Leader's Lasting Value Is Measured by Succession.

—John C. Maxwell[78]

Most students of leadership recognize John Maxwell as a leadership guru. One of his most basic and important irrefutable laws of leadership is the quote at the beginning of this lesson. In a law firm, day-to-day management tends to limit the time available for strategy and planning, and the time that is available for this important process is often devoted to the midterm of five to seven years in the future. Because succession may be farther down the road, usually at an undetermined date, firm leaders generally spend even less time on it.

After about nine years of leading my firm as its managing partner, I asked myself whether my firm was ready for the future—a future where present practice leaders will desire to retire and present managing leaders will desire to transition out of those positions. Because I realized that the firm was not really ready, I felt challenged to find a way for our firm to transition firm practices and leadership in an orderly way, to assure a successful organization well after the present members were of counsel, or retired. We embarked on a succession planning process and discovered it needed to be, like all strategy and planning, perpetual. Through this process I identified five basic questions law firm leaders must ask themselves about their firm's readiness for succession and their own role in assuring the firm is always ready for transition.

---

77. This lesson is based on the author's article "Five Questions to Ask about Your Firm's Succession Readiness," *Law Practice Magazine* 37, no. 3 (May/June 2011).
78. *The 21 Irrefutable Laws of Leadership,* page 215.

Leadership Thought and Application

How do we define *succession*, or what exactly are we planning for? In a perfect world, succession planning is truly a subset of a law firm's overall strategic plan. A law firm should always be concerned with its markets, competition, and substantive talent. Leaders should always be concerned with the need for a plan to sustain the firm over the long term. As reflected in a typical compensation system, the tendency of most law firms is to emphasize short-term success. Because of this focus, firm owners usually do not think too much about succession. In fact, it may become an afterthought, something that needs minimal attention so the firm can get through a crisis. As a result, many firm owners and leaders do not really understand what it means to plan for succession. When they do begin to plan for succession, firm leaders often realize that they have not considered succession as a part of the broader comprehensive plan, and they may have difficulty narrowly defining their present succession issues. Consequently the firm's ability to develop a narrowly tailored plan will likely be compromised. Properly defined, however, the resulting succession plan might be successfully incorporated into the overall firm strategic plan and become a key component, subject to accountability processes and regular follow-up. If firm leaders do not have a narrowly focused definition, the process can send them off on tangents that are already addressed in the firm's larger strategic plan; for example, partner compensation, marketing, and practice group development, which may already have more narrowly focused plans for change and development. The definition of *succession* may not be the same for each organization, but every law firm should consider the following three main categories in the process:

1. **Firm growth.** How large should the firm be? Does the firm need to grow into new areas of substantive practice? Do clients or potential clients have unmet needs that the firm should address? Does the firm need to expand any of its

existing substantive service areas? Should the firm expand geographically, and if so, should that expansion be virtual or physical?

2. **Practice succession.** What are we going to do as members of our firm age? What process can we use to transition substantive work from the older generation to the younger? How can we make our older generation comfortable with transition processes and assure them that the firm will not ungratefully cast them aside once the work has been delegated? How can firm leaders encourage firm members to discuss their life plans and expectations honestly and openly and to regularly update others as their plans change?

3. **Management planning.** Do we have a plan for management succession that allows responsibility to shift from existing managers to future managers? Do we have a process for identifying future leaders of the firm? Does the firm have a plan for developing leadership in others?

Are we dealing with a succession crisis now, and if not, do we need to plan before we do? Many law firm owners do not consider succession planning until a crisis is upon them. At that point, action is called for, and the time to prepare is limited, increasing the likelihood of making a mistake. If a firm is not in the midst of a succession crisis, timing considerations will likely determine whether the firm begins to plan. Most often, firms without a current leadership void or pending retirements defer succession planning. Although some situations present a clearer need than others, I would suggest that any firm without a succession plan actually does have a crisis. Certainly a law firm with new leadership and no significant leader nearing retirement seems to have less of a need for succession planning. But none of us know what tomorrow may bring, and a retirement, death, or burnout of a leader might occur at any time. Further, and on the brighter side, an opportunity for growth may arise and be successfully pursued if a succession plan is in place. The need for a succession plan is important and should be raised and discussed with firm owners. Owners need to realize that without a succession plan the firm is in crisis mode (in most cases without even knowing it). Unless a leader raises this topic and fully vets it among firm stakeholders, most firm members will assume there is no crisis, until the crisis becomes an immediate need.

Should we ask a third party to facilitate our succession planning, and if so, how do we pick one? The answer might depend on how Firm leaders answer the question of whether or not a succession "crisis" is being experienced by the Firm (or is fast approaching). Although any firm without a succession plan is in a crisis, decisions about succession planning are often based on probability. For example, if a firm has newer and younger leadership, leaders may feel that it has more opportunity to address succession planning within its regularly scheduled comprehensive strategic planning. If this is the case, the decision to retain a succession planning consultant may be made in connection with the decision to hire a facilitator for the whole strategic planning process. The first time a law firm engages in strategic planning, a consultant may be helpful. If succession planning is incorporated into an existing strategic planning process, it may fit well into the established planning process, which might not involve a facilitator other than existing firm management. However, if firm leaders perceive that the firm has a critical succession crisis, hiring a consultant with as much experience as possible in the area of succession planning is strongly encouraged. Certainly it is possible for a firm to handle a critical succession crisis on its own, but succession planning involves examining difficult truths. An impartial, experienced professional is generally more able to find a way to tell firm owners what they need to hear but do not want to hear. And hearing these truths from a consultant is generally much easier than from a firm leader. A consultant can also help firm members learn how to make succession decisions now and in the future.

The impartial and competent consultant can raise difficult questions and make firm members uncomfortable because he or she is only motivated by a job well done (and the referral business that may come from a successful engagement). The consultant knows that regardless of the content of the advice given, he or she will go home (likely to another town or state) at the end of the consultation. When firm members handle the succession planning process, often those things that need to be said will go unspoken. The decision not to use a consultant is usually based on finances, and in many cases the law firm is being penny-wise and pound-foolish about its future.

Which people from the firm should we involve in the succession planning process? Deciding whom to include is always a difficult issue. The firm's definition of *succession* affects whether the process is confidential and restricted to owners or whether nonowners, such as staff and associates, should be involved. If a consultant is hired, he or she will have a recommendation after inquiring about whether, or to what extent, nonowners are involved in other decision making. Firms that are generally more open about information and decision making may want to consider the same degree of openness in the succession planning process. Otherwise the process may not be as successful. Firms that are generally less open might be able to limit the process to owners, but they may also be limiting their success. Generally nonowners have diverse views on a variety of organizational issues, and their input should be encouraged because broader information generally improves leadership's decision-making. Because succession planning is such an important process, at a minimum firms are advised to incorporate a mechanism that explains the process and gathers views and information from associates, practice group staff, and administrative personnel.

What should firm leadership do to assure success in the process? Firm leaders should bring enthusiastic support and shared involvement to the process. Their support and buy-in does not necessarily assure success, but without their support, failure is guaranteed. The process should not be controlled or dictated by the managing partner, the management committee, or the most-senior owners. Instead, leadership, responsibility, and significant involvement in the process should be shared among diverse members within the ownership group, and perhaps senior associates approaching ownership status. In addition, a diverse committee should recommend consultants, negotiate a time line for the process, and be responsible for garnering significant owner support within practice groups. This committee should include representatives from different practice groups, some members of management, and younger and older owners.

Succession planning is definitely one component of strategic planning on which a law firm needs to spend time. The process is necessary, but it can be a significant financial burden on a law firm. The firm must properly define *succession*, identify the desired result of succession planning, and detail the means for achieving that result. With that information, succession planning can help make the firm's substantive practice, governance, and desired growth a reality.

Questions to Ponder

- Does your firm have a strategic plan? Does it include comprehensive succession planning?
- What aspect of succession planning outlined in this chapter do you find most difficult to plan? Most difficult to implement?
- Do you find it difficult to sell your followers on hiring a consultant to help with the process of planning? How do you feel about hiring consultants to help in these types of processes?
- Do you involve more than just firm owners in your planning processes? If not, why not? Do you feel that succession planning is a different higher-level type of planning that should be limited to owners?

Suggested Reading

John C. Maxwell, *The 21 Irrefutable Laws of Leadership* (Nashville: Thomas Nelson, 1998).

J.W. Marriott, Jr. and Kathi Ann Brown, *The Spirit to Serve: Marriott's Way* (New York: HarperCollins, 1997).

LESSON 35 PLANNING FOR GROWTH

Effective leaders must blend history and precedent with wisdom from the past, applying them to emerging realities.

—Harold Myra and Marshall Shelley[79]

Leaders of successful law firms need to be prepared for common circumstances such as these that arise from time to time:

1. Leaders of another firm approach management about the possibility of a merger.
2. A practice group or member presents a perceived opportunity for expanding the firm in some way, such as providing legal services in a new substantive practice area, hiring additional professional staff, or opening an office in another geographic location.

I recently heard the story of a midsize firm that was approached by another midsize firm in a neighboring state to discuss the possibility of a merger. The firm that was approached revealed that it had no plan for expansion and growth. It had a firm-wide strategic plan, but it lacked one very important aspect—succession planning, including proposals for the firm's future growth and sustainability. The strategic plan did not include any process for vetting new practice areas or strategic opportunities that might arise. Neither did it delegate to any group in the firm the obligation to evaluate opportunities, other than already burdened executive committee. The firm simply did not understand how important it was to ask some very important questions, such as the following:

- Should the firm expand in the future, and if so, to what extent?
- If the firm should expand, should it be done through the hiring of recently graduated law students or laterals, or

---
[79]. *The Leadership Secrets of Billy Graham*, page 303.

should the firm attempt to consolidate with other smaller firms?
- Should the firm seek to be merged into a larger law firm, and if so, how would the firm evaluate such an opportunity?
- Should the firm expand its service areas geographically, substantively, or both?

The leaders of this firm met with the leaders of the firm that had approached them, considered the opportunity, and then met with their own partners. The idea of a merger was discussed but without any direction. When the questions of compatible practice areas and firm cultures were discussed, members had difficulty identifying significant characteristics of the culture of either firm. Partners who were not very interested in the opportunity threw up road blocks to further discussion, indicating their perception that the two firms' practice areas were not compatible and the transition would be much too difficult to undergo successfully. By the end of the meeting, it was clear that the leaders could not respond to the strategic opportunity. They had not established a process or plan for dealing with such inquiries, a plan that would provide owners with information and a well-thought-out recommendation.

Leadership Thought and Application

As stated previously, a major role of any law firm leader is substantial involvement in strategic planning. That planning must necessarily consider issues related to firm growth, practice area growth, growth in numbers, and growth in the geographic areas it serves (whether physically or across historically recognized boundaries through use of technology).

Have a plan. Every law firm needs a multifaceted growth plan. Certainly the amount of work involved in developing and executing a succession growth plan is much more than one person can handle. In addition, succession plans, especially those that might involve such difficult or sensitive issues as mergers and hiring, need to be backed by a team of leaders within the firm who are responsible for developing a plan's action points and trusted to obtain the necessary buy-in of other firm stakeholders. A succession growth plan needs many different components, including most of the following:

1. **Client and service development.** Development is not just about marketing, though marketing needs to be a substantial part of the activities that are pursued. In many firms, marketing consists of a committee that focuses on spending sums of money on advertising, charitable donations, and a yellow pages ad. The committee usually organizes firm get-togethers with local businesses or organizations identified as referral sources. It also assures that firm members attend a requisite number of client lunches, charity golf tournaments or community events each month. Certainly someone needs to consider these types of opportunities; however, client development should be so much more. The firm leader needs to assure that client development is not limited to a marketing committee but that each and every member of the firm is involved. Every individual lawyer needs a well-thought-out plan for client development as part of his or her individual practice development plan, and that plan must be integrated into a practice group plan if the firm has practice groups. The individual and practice group plans must also be consistent with the firm's client development goals and objectives. Each practice group plan, or for smaller firms the overall firm plan, should include periodic evaluation of possible expansion into new substantive service areas.

2. **Client retention.** The firm leader is responsible for assuring that the organization has a mechanism to make sure that clients are very satisfied with the legal services they receive and the manner in which they are provided. Because many

types of legal representation are unlike commodities, the process as well as the result are important to the client. A firm needs regular client feedback systems, which will not be effective unless the firm also has a process for delivering client comments to each individual attorney, and accountability to assure that concerns are addressed. In the past, conducting client surveys was time-consuming and expensive. Today, inexpensive online tools that use e-mail or extranets can be used for client surveys. Firm leaders should consider making visits to clients for the purpose of maintaining a quality relationship. There truly is no substitute for personal face to face contact, with an expression of concern and care for the client. Accountability with each service provider in the firm should also be a significant part of any client retention system. Once feedback content is gathered, the leader must assure that the firm has a system to provide positive feedback to the provider. The best system will have regular personal meetings between the leader and provider, including lawyers and staff members (such as paralegals) who have direct client contact.

3. **Personal development plans.** Each member of the firm should have a comprehensive personal development plan that includes a strategy to develop and maintain clients and a personal leadership development program. Each member of the firm needs to strive to become a leader of others who, in turn, will someday develop into leaders. Specific programs will vary depending on each individual's strengths and weaknesses; however, each plan needs to have the goal of developing a well-rounded and mature professional leader. In firms with practice groups, a practice group leader needs to monitor the progress of each individual group member and assure that progress is made. In firms without practice groups, a member of firm management should do this job.

There is no recommended template or form book for these plans; they need to be crafted individually. Many consultants can help create these personalized plans. One program that helps young lawyers develop these plans is the Young Lawyers Leadership Academy of the Center for Creative Leadership. (For more information about this and the center's other lawyer leadership programs, see http://www.ccl.org/leadership/landing/legal/client.aspx.)

4. **Evaluation of strategic opportunities.** An area of great weakness in most firms is the ability to evaluate strategic opportunities, including mergers and other possibilities for growth. Because firms are generally ill prepared for evaluation, they either leap before they look, so failure is more likely, or they do not pursue a great opportunity because they have cold feet. Every law firm leader hopes and desires that followers will trust the leader's actions and recommendations. Because of the typical organizational structure of a law firm, however, every leader should have a policy or mechanism in place to assure that the firm will respond to strategic opportunities when they arise. A plan for evaluating these opportunities might include the following:

   a. **A specific procedure for response to inquiries.** For instance, other firm owners will want to know how management will respond to inquiries. The procedure may include an overall goal of the firm in making any response, such as in this example:

   > "One goal of the Firm is to enhance the value of the organization to its shareholders. Accordingly, Management will review all strategic opportunities with a view toward long-term enhancement of the Firm as an organization, and each of the shareholder's position in it."

The procedure should include a definition of what constitutes a strategic opportunity and the specific action steps that will be taken by leaders in the initial response, such as:

> All inquiries, offers, or expressions of interest with respect to any Strategic Opportunity shall be reported immediately to the Management Committee. No other director of the Firm shall initiate any such discussions or respond to any inquiries without the prior express direction of the Management Committee. The general content of a proper response to any inquiry with respect to a Strategic Opportunity by anyone other than Management should be consistent with the following:

> *'Thank you for your inquiry. The firm is following an existing long-term strategic plan, but is always interested in opportunities that may lead to the long-term enhancement of our law firm, its service to clients, and each of the Firm's shareholders and employees as well. The Firm's Management Committee is responsible for analyzing and reviewing all such opportunities and making a recommendation regarding any specific opportunity to the full Board of Directors of the Firm. It would be inappropriate for me to investigate such an opportunity independently. Accordingly, if you would like, I will bring your opportunity to the attention of the Firm's Management Committee. At that point, we will let you know if the Firm is interested in discussing the opportunity further.'*

b. **General evaluation parameters.** Initially, firm leaders should establish parameters that they will use to determine, for instance, the viability of a potential merger candidate. Rather than finding out at the end of the process that a prospective law firm is inappropriate, a set of overriding general parameters creates a guide for screening candidate firms at the beginning of the process. These general parameters help firm leadership determine whether to ask the other firm for additional information. Firm management should determine and approve the parameters, including such areas as: specialization, profitability, demographic of client base, billing rate disparity, size of employee base, and firm reputation.

c. **Merger objectives.** It is important for the firm leader to explain to owners the reasons for considering a merger and the goals desired to be achieved through the merger, and the leader needs to get the owners' agreement. Both entities in a merger or acquisition will have separate reasons, but the final goals should be shared; therefore, leaders should know beforehand how these will be expressed.

d. **Substantive considerations.** As management evaluates opportunities, it must consider factors such as these:
- enhanced competitive position
- complementary practices and increased specialization
- geographic expansion
- stability
- improved client base
- improved compensation
- expanded substantive services for clients.

e. **Additional information.** If you decide to move forward with an opportunity, consider gathering or exchanging the following information:
- firm history
- practice areas and client representation
- reasons another firm is considering a merger
- firm's strengths and weaknesses
- synopsis of governance structure and legal structure
- explanation of practice management systems or departments

5. **Hiring plan.** The strategic opportunity process noted above is generally about opportunities from the outside, most notably a potential merger. Some firms will grow by merger; however, other firms are more interested in growth that comes from hiring individual lawyers. Hiring opportunities may come directly from law schools, the court system, another firm (lateral practitioners), or government or business. Firm leaders need to assure that the owners understand how the firm will sustain itself in the future. Depending on the firm's size, leadership should consider assigning oversight of the hiring function to a single leader. If the firm has practice groups, the leader assigned to coordinate the hiring process should work closely with practice group leaders to assure that the staffing needs of practice groups are satisfied. A valuable hiring plan includes short-term (one to two years) goals as well as a consistent statement (and periodic restatement) of the firm vision for growth and future firm size.

Adjust the governance structure. The structure of a law firm needs to facilitate growth. First, a firm that is large enough to have practice groups is large enough to have a committee whose primary task is succession planning and growth. This committee should not only be responsible for developing plans and recommendations, but for implementation. Second, the initial process of planning for succession and growth needs to define, or redefine if needed, all of the firm's management or governance positions so that it is clear who in the firm is responsible for handling the substantive work of management and leadership, including making decisions about responding to strategic opportunities. Third, there must be a good rotation system for management positions so all practice groups and all levels of firm members have some role in the process. A rotation system goes a long way in gaining well-rounded support for the recommendations that firm leaders eventually make.

Communication and involvement. Law firms are generally very "tight lipped" about their plans for substantive growth. Confidentiality makes sense in these types of matters mostly because the legal environment is increasingly competitive. Although a few members from all levels of the firm are involved in the decision making process, the entire firm needs to be aware of any developments well before the public. You don't want anyone learning about changes in the firm from a newspaper or other outside source. Further, because growth and sustainability have a significant impact on the firm's future, the firm leader needs to assure that the younger generation of the firm is well-informed about any plans or developments in this area and included as a significant part of the process. It is crucial that the younger generation of the firm buys in the plans for growth. Lawyers in the firm's younger generation are much less likely to move on to the perceived greener pastures of another firm if they are given a meaningful part in the process of planning their firm's growth.

Questions to Ponder

- Does your firm have a plan for growth? Is it documented? Has it been approved or agreed to in some way by the members of the firm?
- Does your firm governance structure facilitate growth? If not, what changes need to be made? Does your firm need a succession planning committee?
- How well do you communicate the plans for the firm's future to its members? Do you include nonowner members of the firm, such as younger lawyers and select staff, in the planning process?

Suggested Reading

Harold Myra and Marshall Shelley, *The Leadership Secrets of Billy Graham* (Grand Rapids, MI: Zondervan, 2005).

Larry Bossidy and Ram Charan, *Execution: The Discipline of Getting Things Done* (New York: Crown Business, 2002).

LESSON 36 PLANNING FOR RETIREMENT—SUCCESSION OF A PRACTICE

The ability to develop capable successors is a hallmark of great leaders. Ultimately, if your people can't do it without you, you haven't been successful in raising up other leaders.

—Ken Blanchard and Mark Miller[80]

I have a friend who is in a law practice with one other partner. They have several staff members, paralegals, legal assistants, and administrative staff. Their firm has become very successful in only a few years. My friend is in his midthirties, and his partner is in his upper sixties. They are a true equal partnership and have become successful due to the way they use team principles in much of what they do in leading clients and leading their firm. The older partner has recently announced that he plans to exit the practice; in less than a year. Although the day-to-day firm leadership has been very effective for clients and firm members, these two partners have not planned for the future. They have let each other down, and they have let down the nonlawyer members of their firm who rely on the firm for employment.

The announcement comes, at a time when, due to other commitments, my friend has very little time to coordinate and execute everything that needs to be done. My friend is now considering the likelihood that he and his partner will simply close the practice within the year. The elder partner will head to a new retirement community in Florida. My friend will likely head to the grind of a large firm where he will live under a new set of rules and expectations and where he will give up the entrepreneurial excitement of being the leader of a very successful small law firm. What the future holds for my friend has created in him some sense of panic. This

---

80. *The Secret*, page 113.

panic is almost entirely a result of failing to plan for the elder partner's future retirement in such a way that the firm could continue as an organization. The most difficult part of closing the firm is that several people will lose their jobs at a time when employment in that area of the country is very difficult to find.

Early in my tenure as managing partner, I was challenged with the pending retirement of an established partner and leader. The firm had no succession planning to speak of. Time was short, but not as short as in my friend's dilemma. Fortunately, the continued existence of my firm was not at stake, but at the same time, it was an established practice with a huge client base in jeopardy. We had no plan for moving my partner's client files and matters to the younger generation. As in many other firms, this retiring partner had guardedly protected his client base for many years. Though he had delegated work to younger lawyers, it was never to the extent that a client would feel comfortable in a routine direct relationship with a partner or associate from the younger generation. Our leadership dilemma was to develop a transition plan to move billable work to the next generation, assign specific lawyers to maintain client relationships, and assure that the retiring partner made client introductions during the transition. Fortunately, the retiring partner had a true "firm-first" attitude toward this process, even though he had been very protective of his client relationships in the past. Subsequent to that retirement, we recognized the importance of comprehensive succession planning, and the firm began a process to develop a plan that includes retirement and practice succession. As of this writing, it is a work in progress.

Leadership Thought and Application

The law firm leader has a significant role in assuring that the firm plans for retirement and practice succession and implements these plans appropriately. A leader should not be surprised by an announcement that a firm lawyer is retiring or leaving for some other reason. Certainly planning for medical emergencies is much more difficult, but otherwise the loss of a lawyer's or key staff member's contribution should not be a surprise. The long-term viability of a law firm depends upon this type of planning and preparedness. Here are some of the principles of this form of succession planning to consider:

Consistent firm-wide planning. As stated in other lessons in this chapter, succession planning must be a part of the firm-wide strategic plan. Often firm leaders do not realize its importance until they are faced with an event that has escalated into a crisis because the firm had no plan. Of course, the firm may need to address any pending crisis first, but eventually succession must be addressed. The need for each lawyer to have an individual professional development plan that addresses business and marketing is also discussed in this chapter. Succession planning must also be a part of these individual plans. The individual plan needs to be comprehensive because it is a plan for the full lifetime of the lawyer while with the firm. All individual plans are living, breathing documents, and they also must be consistent with the firm-wide plans and with each other. Consistency and the comprehensive "lifetime of the lawyer" nature of each individual's plan encourage loyalty. Loyalty is even more likely if each member sees the connection between his or her individual plan, the firm's plan, and other individuals' lifetime plans.

The overall firm succession plan should require that before a new member is hired, firm leaders or its hiring partner should propose an individual plan that addresses succession. These individual plans should be initially approved (or adopted) shortly after employment, and they should also include provisions for initial business (client) development, professional development in maintenance of client relationships, training in originating and delegating client work, and a long transition period prior to anticipated retirement so that succession does not become a crisis. Obviously, a new associate in the firm will not necessarily know when he or she will retire, and issues may certainly arise to change the course of a professional life. This is the reason, however, that the plan develops and evolves with the individual.

Appropriate length. The firm's plan needs to provide an appropriate amount of time for practice succession and client transitioning, and a four-year transition period is recommended. If the transition is shorter, a client is more likely to be dissatisfied and look to another source for legal service. Because an individual professional development plan is personalized for each lawyer, firm leaders should frequently check with each member to determine where he or she is on the professional time line in the plan. When it appears that an individual lawyer is about four years from retirement, leaders need to encourage that the transition of client matters begin. This is not just about delegation of work (which should always be encouraged) but the transition of client relationships to the younger generation.

Crisis plan. Within every succession plan, the firm needs to consider the possibility of disability or death of a valued and productive firm member. Obviously this situation can occur at any stage of life, leaving a huge vacuum for the firm. Just as every firm should have a disaster plan for a crime or natural disaster, every firm needs a plan for a lawyer's sudden death, disability, or other temporary or permanent interruption in the lawyer's work. The plan should address client needs and quickly transition all clients to other lawyers in firm. Further, because most firm members have nonbillable duties to take care of on a regular basis (or they should), the crisis plan should designate a member of the firm, whether administrative or management, to assure that these important tasks are carried out.

Fairness in planning for retirement or of counsel status. Transitioning clients can certainly be difficult for a retiring lawyer, and if the compensation system too heavily penalizes the retiring lawyer, the transition may not be effective. A part of the overall firm-wide succession planning process needs to incorporate assurances that the lawyer who is willing to move matters to younger generations is not penalized by formula-based compensation that largely considers individual production, such as client receipts or profitability. Leaders need to assure that the lawyer who is transitioning will be respected for long service to the firm. If the lawyer is transitioning between full-time status and retirement, for example in an of counsel role, the firm should give some substance to that role. In many cases a highly productive past rainmaker might have a compensable rainmaking role while the transition is being completed. In any event, leaders need to proactively make a retiring partner feel comfortable with this new stage in life and feel that he or she continues to be valuable to the firm. The alternative is that the retiring partner will not be forthcoming about his or her plans and will guardedly protect and work up client files until he or she announces retirement and walks away with very short notice.

Questions to Ponder

- Have you had any retirements in your firm in the past ten years? How did you handle client transitions? How did the firm treat the retiring partner? Do you believe that the retiring partner felt that the process was respectful?
- Does your firm have a strategic plan? Does it incorporate succession planning? Do firm members have individual professional development plans, and are they comprehensive? Does each one include plans for retirement and transition of the member's practice to the younger generation? If not, how should the plans be revised?
- What process do you have in place for the death or disability of a member? Do you have a crisis plan in place that will address all client and administrative issues? If you do, is it comprehensive? If you do not, what specific policies and

procedures do you need to have in writing in the event of such a crisis?

- Does your compensation plan work against effective implementation of retirement succession planning? Is there a drastic financial disincentive to a partner approaching retirement? What changes does your firm need to make to its compensation plan to encourage retirement planning that effectively transitions client work to the younger generation?

Suggested Reading

Ken Blanchard and Mark Miller, *The Secret* (San Francisco: Berret-Koehler, 2004).

Jim Collins, *How the Mighty Fall and Why Some Companies Never Give In* (New York: Harper-Collins, 2009).

LESSON 37 PLANNING FOR MANAGEMENT SUCCESSION

> *Keeping the choice of my successor was the easy part. But that was the only easy thing about it. Making the pick was not only the most important decision of my career, it was the most difficult and agonizing one I ever had to make. It damn near drove me crazy, causing many sleepless nights.*
>
> — Jack Welch with John A. Byrne[81]

One of the best examples of leadership succession is the process that Jack Welch employed in choosing a future leader of General Electric in the 1990s. In his book *Jack: Straight from the Gut*, he describes the process. Certainly his method will not work in a law firm because law firms do not have the same type of top-down leadership system as General Electric. However, the basic objectives are universal. Welch began identifying candidates years in advance. He and a small group of leaders put together a list of objectives, such as choosing the strongest leader, finding the best mix of corporate executive officer skills, and providing an acceptable transition time. Welch indicates that his goal was not just to find a single leader, but to leave General Electric with the best possible team of leaders.

As a contrast, I have seen something very different in many law firms, especially in smaller firms led for many years by a trusted benevolent dictator. Those who follow this type of leader, primarily partners, are fairly well satisfied with management, or they are too frightened to say anything about it. The leader enjoys his position and is fairly good at dealing with finance and staff issues and generally keeping the peace. The managing partner does not really have a management committee, or if there is one, it is really not a team. Through the years, good management parades as good leadership,

---

81. *Jack: Straight from the Gut*, page 407.

but truly it is not. A key component of excellent leadership is succession planning. A leader is really only as good as his or her successor. In this scenario, the managing partner will eventually die or retire. When he does so, his co-owners may or may not have much notice of the upcoming void in the firm. In cases like this, the transition period is almost always shorter than needed. With a lack of notice, succession planning is generally limited to either electing a single person or forming a committee as a replacement for the manager who is leaving. This type of planning is usually just a management solution, and it leaves a huge void when it comes to true leadership.

Leadership Thought and Application

Every leader has the responsibility to plan for the future. Clearly, day-to-day concerns can easily overcome leaders. Regardless, an adequate amount of time and resources must be found to plan for the future—not just figuring out where the firm is heading but also who is going to lead it or how the firm will choose who will lead. Those presently in management positions of a firm need to consider several actions to help assure success in management and leadership succession.

Develop leadership capability. Development of leadership should not be limited. Every law firm needs to provide leadership tools to all members and encourage them to develop the following capabilities:

1. Lead staff and others
2. Be leaders in all of the communities (local, professional, and civic) of which they are a part
3. Lead clients
4. Lead the firm

Leaders need to develop systems to identify members who have these capabilities. Members who are the best fit for law firm leadership might be identified through these intrafirm systems:

1. **Education sessions.** Firm leadership might create specific leadership training and development programs. Depending upon the size of the firm, the sessions might be in-house or outside the firm. Several law schools have created leadership education programs for members of law firms. For example, the Center for Creative Leadership (www.ccl.org) in Greensboro, North Carolina, has created a comprehensive set of programs for lawyers, including Young Lawyers Leadership Academy, Leadership Development for Lawyer-Leaders, Coaching Services for Lawyers, and Leading Lawyer Teams for Impact. In addition, every firm should establish general leadership training sessions for all lawyers and staff. Preferably these sessions should be informal and accessible to all members, and they should also be fun, collaborative, and interactive.

2. **Strategic project teams.** In most cases, the majority of a lawyer's work is done between a single client and a single lawyer. When firm members work in teams, leadership skills can often be identified. Firm leaders can establish strategic project teams so professionals can work collaboratively and move forward with firm strategy. These teams allow firm leaders to assign specific tasks to individuals so the leaders can determine which members might have what it takes to be a part of future leadership.

3. **Practice group structure.** Teams of members within the same practice group are another way to identify and develop future leaders. Practice group teams might be established as follows:

    a. Leadership of the team rotates among members, which can help identify members with particular skills.

b. Through the practice group structure, all members are held accountable to a comprehensive business practice and leadership plan, including a system for objective evaluations and assessments.

c. The practice group is itself well-defined, and a specific job description for the leader is used to evaluate members' performance while they are in the leadership role.

d. Practice group leaders are held accountable to firm leadership through periodic reporting, and the accountability is based on their leadership efforts and the performance of each member of his or her group. Existing practice group leadership needs to be consulted to identify present members who might take over as leaders of the practice group in the future.

Compensation. Existing leadership needs to address appropriate compensation for future managers and leaders. If present leadership makes compensation changes, others in the firm may perceive the change as self-serving, so leaders will need to consider this in making recommendations. Management compensation plans and deciding how to approach compensation issues are topics that are beyond the scope of this book. All firm owner groups, however, need to fully understand that the firm will get only the leadership it is willing to pay for. Succession planning must include bold initiatives to assure that compensation of firm management and leadership reflects the fact that these functions are the most important in any law firm.

Management succession group. A law firm needs to establish entities within the firm that are accountable for implementing the firm's leadership education plan and identify members with the greatest ability to lead in the future. Firms should consider creating a permanent committee to deal with succession issues (including management succession, succession of individual practices, and succession of the firm's substantive work). The membership of this committee should rotate in such a way that all the generations of lawyers in the firm are represented. If members of staff are not included on this committee, their regular input should certainly be sought.

Questions to Ponder

- Is the present leadership of your firm prepared for change? For retirement? For the future? Is the present leader receptive to considering the future and succession? If you are the present leader, how do you feel about this concept?
- What type of plan does your firm have for training members to be leaders? Does the plan include any mechanisms for identifying future leaders?
- Does the firm have a system that adequately compensates firm leaders? Does the firm compensate billable work more than management and leadership time? If so, how do you plan to convince qualified candidates to accept leadership and management positions in the firm?

Suggested Reading

Jack Welch with John A. Byrne, *Jack: Straight from the Gut* (New York: Warner Books, 2001).

Mark Sanborn, *The Fred Factor: Every Person's Guide to Making the Ordinary Extraordinary* (Mechanicsburg, PA: Executive Books, 2002).

Peter Giuliani, *Passing the Torch Without Getting Burned* (Chicago: American Bar Association, 2013).

Conclusion

I believe that the principles discussed in this book are easy to understand. Although they are easily understood, I have learned over twelve years of leading and managing a law firm that they are very difficult to implement. Further, given the many uncertainties and demands of life, a person entrusted with a position of authority may have difficulty accepting that studying and applying leadership principles will actually increase success and improve relationships in a law firm. Without personal discipline, the emergencies of the day will always be more important than learning and applying leadership principles, which may have no tangible results for months or years. When I organized the contents of this book, I chose short lessons in the hope that readers would devote a very short time *each day* to reading and studying leadership principles so that their firms might achieve greater organizational success.

Exemplary leadership does not come overnight or in a week; it is a journey of successes and failures. Through regular study of these lessons, I hope that you might recall what you have learned when faced with opportunities that test your leadership. True leadership comes through hard work and diligent effort. I wish you well on your journey.

Index

A

A Few Good Men, movie, 167–168
Above the Law, website, 196
Abuse, workplace, 184–186
Academic programs, self education, 69–70
Accomplishments, former leaders and, 110
Accountability
    coaching relationships, 61–62
    establishing mutual, 120
    team work, 23
Achievement, shared, 121–123
Actions
    leadership and, 6
    regular, principle of, 12
Active listening, 83–84
Activities, servant leadership, 12
Administrators, loss of, 212
Admiration, learning and, 108
Aligning, principle of, 127–128
Allen, James, 72
Alone time, 88–89
Ambition, directed, 113
Andrews, Andy, 50
Armerding, Hudson T., 66
Associates, loss of, 213
Attitude, leadership, 17, 213–214

Attorneys, recruitment and education, 32, 174–175
Authentic voice, finding, 124–128
Authority
    discretionary, teamwork and, 23
    methods of, 120–121
    power and, 3–4
    respect for lines of, 147
Autonomy, 39, 134–164
Availability, clients and, 170
Axiom, 42

B

Baker Donelson Law firm, 112–113
Bakke, Dennis, 118
Balance, 72–73
Be My Guest, 101–102
Behavior, positive, contagious, 130–131
Bespoke client services, 169, 209
Bias, addressing, 152
Big picture thinking, 88
Billing, late, 76
Bissette, Lou, 168–169
Blanchard, Ken, 10–11, 238
Blanchard, Kenneth, 188
Bossidy, Larry, 55

Bradberry, Travis, 99
Brobeck, Phelger & Harrison, collapse of, 36–37
Bullying, 184–186
Business models, flaws in, 36
Business relationships, clients and, 170
Busyness, 77–78
Byrne, John A., 244

C

Calmness of mind, 72, 214–217
Capable leadership, developing, 245
Carroll, Ken, 43–44
Casting vision, 199–201
Center for Creative Leadership, 69–70, 176
Change, initiating, courage and, 142
Character, leadership and, 27
Characteristics, leadership, 11
Charan, Ram, 55
Churchill, Winston, 129
Circumstances, guided by, 77
CLE leadership programs, 176
Client development, planning, 230
Clients
    changing philosophies and, 42
    demands, changing, 46
    feedback systems, 231
    influence and, 165–166
    pitfalls, common, 170
    relations, leadership and, 165–177
    relationships, maintaining, 231
    retention of, planning, 230–231
    teams, 183
Coaching
    characteristics of, 61–62
    coaches, 59–65
    defined, 60
    diversity and, 100
    former leaders and, 109
    ground rules, 64
    professional, 59–60
Collaboration
    governance, 31–32
    importance of, 4
    instituting systems of, 184
Collaborative tools, electronic, 45

Collegiality, business reality, 53
Collins, Jim, 36, 55, 113
Comfort level, 24, 130–131
Commitment, 18, 203–205
Common interests, teamwork and, 23
Common missions, 2
Communication, 110
    changes in, 34
    clients and, 170
    conciliatory conflict resolution, 162–164
    e-mail, guidelines, 82
    individual attention and, 81–82
    interfirm, 45
    leadership and, 80–85
    nonaccusatory statements, 84
    teamwork and, 184
Compensation plans, 209, 222, 247
Complementary strengths and weaknesses, 23–24
Conciliatory conflict resolution, 162–164
Conduct
    objectively appropriate, 149
    professional, 188–194
    unacceptable, 141
Confidence
    courageous action and, 24–25
    feelings of in presence of leader, 129
    infectious, Winston Churchill, 129
    lack of, 76
Conflicts
    avoidance of, 161–164
    confronting with courage, 138–140
    dealing with, 161–164
    ownership of outcome, 181
Confrontation
    conciliatory conflict resolution, 162–164
    courage and, 138–140
Consistency, trust and, 16–17
Consultants, 41, 224–225
Contributions, recognition of, 146
Controlling leadership, risks of, 14–15
Core competencies, pathfinding and, 127
Core values, fun, promoting, 119
Counsel status, fairness planning, 241–242

Courage
   acts of, 24–25
   admitting when wrong, 142
   crisis and, 211–217
   discipline of, 141–143
   foundation of trust in leadership, 138–143
   saying no, 75, 142
Covey, Stephen R., 53, 76–77, 124–128
Covey's leadership model, 126–128
Credibility, 171, 198
Crisis
   action and, 214–217
   blessing of, 214
   defined, 212
   examples of, 121–123
   leadership through, 211–220
   opportunities, finding, 216
   planning for, 214–217
   reaction, leadership, 214–217
   succession planning and, 223–224
Criticism, perceived public, 161–164
Crocker, H. W. III, 103
Customer Think blog, 55–56
Customers, connecting with, 165–177

D

Deaths, crisis of, 213
Decision, making, structures of, 181–182
Decisions
   gauging, 108
   low trust environments, 136
   numbers and, 188
   supporting, 24
   teamwork and, 24
Dees, Morris, 66–67
Defeat, worse things than, 103
Delegation
   action and, 24
   avoidance of, 75–76
   Dwight D. Eisenhower and, 21
   failure to, 95
   firm members, 22–24
   leadership teams and, 20–26
   steps toward, 95
Depree, Max, 54
Depression, Great, 27–28

Determination, leadership and, 36
Development, personal leadership skills, 49–134
Dewey & LeBouf law firm, 36–37, 41
Disasters, crisis of, 213
Discipline, leadership and, 127–128, 156–157
Discussions, teamwork and, 24
Disengagement, stress and, 95
Disney, Walt, 195
Distractions, personal, 76
Diverse management committees, 100
Diversity, 154–155
Dreams, inspiration from, 116
Drucker, Peter F., 97
Dynamics, managing team, 24–25

E

Education, diversity of, 154
Education, leadership
   Center for Creative Leadership, 69–70
   client skills and, 173
   George Washington University programs, 69–70
   meetings and interviews, 70
   opportunities, 175–177
   plan, 66–71
   programs of study, 69–70
   resource list, 68–69
   self discipline and, 68–69
   seminars and events, 69
   through others, 59
   time alone study, 89
Effectiveness, leadership and, 77–78
Egos, channeling, 113
8th Habit, The, 124–125
Eisenhower, Dwight D., 21
Elowitt, Andrew, 60
E-mail, difficult feelings and, 82
Emerging realities, growth and, 228
Employee Empowerment Plan, 120
Empowerment
   autonomy and, 135
   controlling and, 14–19
   origination, 120
   of others, 114

principle of, 128
use of, 2
Encouragement, 38, 114
End of Lawyers, The, 169
Environments, teamwork, fostering, 183–184
Ethical issues, 188–194
Evaluation, mergers, parameters, 233–234
Exemplar Law, LLC, 145
Expectations, changes in, 30–31, 45–46
Expenditures, 159–160

F

Failure
    fear, constant, 104
    large firms and, 41
    law firms, characteristics of, 36–39
    learning from, 105
    opportunities presented by, 102
    ownership of, 105
    plan of response to, 105–106
    precursor, identifying, 105–106
    root causes of, 36–39
    trust and, 103
Fear of failure, 104
Feedback
    alignment principles and, 128
    determining weaknesses and, 99
    regular basis, 149
Female attorney leadership education, 174–175
Firm, expanding, changes in, 32
Firm growth, succession planning, 222–223
Firm leaders, coaching relationships, 60
Firm members, coaching and mentoring, 63–64
First Things First, 76–77
Flitton, Ed, 109
Focus
    graduated, 51
    lack of, 75
    Strategic planning and, 208
Followers
    addressing stray, 39
    disappointment in leadership, 122
    leadership failures and, 38–39
    needing leadership, 214–215
    nurturing, 38
    raising through leadership, 219
    security, sense of, 214–215
    success and, 6
Force, leadership and, 2
Ford, Henry, 82
Form, strategic planning, 208
Former leaders, 109
Fulfillment, 116–133
Fun, leadership and, 118–123
Future, succession and, 219–220

G

General leadership training events, 175
George, Bill, 91
George Washington University programs, 69–70
Gerzon, Mark, 161, 181
Ghani, Usman A., 40
Global economy, law firms and, 208
Goals, 61–62, 211
Good thinkers, 86–87
Goodwin, Doris Kearns, 20
Governance structures, mergers and, 235–236
Gratitude, expressing, importance of, 186
Greaves, Jean, 99
Greene, Robert Michael, 30
Greenleaf, Robert K., quoted, 8
Ground rules, coaching and mentoring, 64
Growth
    communication and, 236
    firm, succession and, 222–223
    mission of, 16
    personal, 66, 93–94, 118
    planning for, 228–237
Guiliani, Rudolph W., 108

H

Habits, principle of good, 11–12
Hands, head, heart, and habits principle, 11–12, 114
Herman Miller, 54
Hierarchy, 33, 132
Hilton, Conrad, 101

Hiring, 40–42, 171, 235
Hodges, Phill, 10–11
Holding ground, courage to, 142
Holistic lifestyle, 93
Honesty, authenticity and, 18
Honeymoon, new leaders and, 4–5
Honoring former leaders, priority of, 109
Hoover, Herbert, 27–28
Hope, exhibiting, 130–131
Hornok, Marcia, 74
Humility, crisis leadership and, 213–214
Hunter, James C., 27
Husband, John, 109

I

Identifying potential leaders, 246–247
Identity, multidimensional, 92–93
Implementation, Strategic planning, 209–210
Influence, 114, 144, 167–168
In-house leadership education, 175
Innovation, in work, 121
Institute for the Future, website, 46
Intentional thinking, 87–88
Interdependence, firm members and, 128
Interests, diversity of, 155
Interruptions, examples of, 94–95
Interventions, bullying and abuse, 184–186
Intimidation, leadership and, 2
Introspection, 99
Involvement, shared values and, 119–120
Issues, coaching relationships, 63–64
Izzo, John, 116–117

J

Jack: Straight from the Gut, 244
Jamison, Steve, 101
Johnansen, Bob, 46
Joy, working with, 117
Joy at Work, 118

K

Klein, Linda, 112–113
Knowledge, clients and, 171

Kouzes, James M., 80
Kubicek, Jeremie, 167

L

LaBarre, Polly, 165
Lateral hiring, 40–42
law firms, failure, characteristics of, 36–39
Lawyers, autonomy and, 135–136
Lawyers, portrayals of, 112
Leader, reasons for becoming, 125
Leadercast training event, 175
Leadership
    admitting when wrong, 142
    boundaries, traversing, 161
    casting vision, 199–201
    character and, 27
    clients, influencing, 165–172
    courage, foundation of trust, 138–143
    Covey's model, 126–128
    daily, 179–194
    empowerment or controlling, 14–19
    failure and, 36–39, 103–104
    finding authentic voice and, 117
    fun, promoting, 118–123
    identifying capabilities, 245–247
    influence, 1
    learning from prior, 102
    non-lawyer, 44
    past models of, 30–35
    personal development plan, 231–232
    personal growth and, 66
    principles, with authority, 148–149
    principles, without authority, 147
    principles of, 114, 126–128
    saying no and, 142
    skills testing, 99
    standing up to others, 142
    succession planning, 219–248
    succession planning, roles in, 225–226
    teamwork, recognition and, 146
    time off, 91–96
    tools, 68–70
    trends affecting, 40–44
    trust, key to, 135
    uniqueness of individuals, 117

Leadership 2.0, 99
Leadership Academy training program, 175–176
Leadership coaches, 59
Leadership teams, 20–26
Leadership Womble Program, 173–174
Legacy, law of, 221
Legal competency, client relations and, 171
Legal service providers, 42
Legalism, binding nature of, 158
Lencioni, Patrick, 135, 211
Life, defining, 92–93
Life experience, diversity of, 154
Lifestyle, vision, reinforcing through, 200–201
Lincoln, Abraham, 20
Listening, empowerment, 17
Listening, active, 83–84
Listening verbalization, 17
Littman, Jonathan, 129
Long range thinking, 88
Lowry, Josh, 55–56
Loyalty, building, qualities of, 24–25
Lundy, Jim, 156
Lyons, Eugene, 27–28

M

Maister, David H., 138, 144, 146, 198
Management
    changes in, 31–34
    defining and acting, 54
    leadership and, 1, 28, 179
    misuse, 3–4
    non-lawyer, 41
    structure, changes in, 31
    succession planning and, 223, 244–248
    time, 74–79
Management succession groups, 247–248
Managerial authority, 190–191
Market, firm's place in, 208
Marketing, realities and pathfinding, 127
Marston, Christopher, 146
Maxwell, John
    360° Leader Comprehensive Assessment, 99

environment, creating, 153
influence, 1
inspiration from dreams, 116
law of legacy, 221
Leadercast training event, 175
leadership as influence, 2
Leadership sucks, 92
potential and thinking, 86–87
universal laws of leadership, 29
McKenna, Patrick, 41, 138
Medill, Joseph, 20
Meetings and interviews, education and, 70
Mentoring, 9, 59–65
Mentors, 51, 62–63
Mergers, 228–229, 232–235
Micromanaging, 15, 114
Miller, Mark, 238
Mission, crisis leadership and, 214
Missions
    common, 2
    defined, 195
    diversity and, 153
    growth, 16
    justifying the plan, 200
    living, personal and business, 126
    shared values and, 119–120
    teamwork and, 183–184
Mistakes
    avoiding the gallows, 5
    significance of, 104, 142
Modeling, principle of, 126
Montgomery, Field Marshall, 129
Morningstar Law Group, 43, 45–46
Motivation, 157–158
Motives
    conciliatory conflict resolution, 162–164
    developing trust and, 141
    fostering trust and, 16
    influence and, 11
Mr. Smith Goes to Washington, movie, 138
Multidimensional identity, 92–93
Mutual submission principle, 131–132
Myers-Briggs personality test, 99
Myra, Harold, 228

N

Naysayers, hijacking, 209
Negative leadership roles, characteristics of, 119
Negative rules and procedures, 159
Nevins, Allan, 28
No, as correct answer, 75, 192
No Grinch Teamwork approach, 146
Noll, Chuck, 144–145
Nonaccusatory statements, 84
Nonbillable functions, 33–34, 190–193
Nonlawyer legal services, change and, 136
Nonverbal signals, observing, 84
Novus Law, 42

O

Open-ended questions, 81–82
Opportunities, crisis, leadership in, 211–212
Organization
    inverting, 10–13
    John Maxwell quoted, 179
    supportive, 182–183
    system, strategic planning and, 205–207
Organizational sharing, importance of, 119
Organizational success, sharing, 121–123
Organized leadership programs, 176
Overturning requests, courage to, 142
Ownership, employee, developing, 15

P

Partiality, leadership and, 149
Partnership, departure of, 212
Passion, 50–52
Pathfinding, principle of, 126–127
Patience with others, 114
Peacemaker, The, 162
Peale, Norman Vincent, 188
People problems, 140–147
Pepper Hamilton law firm, 41
Performance, 56, 157
Personal crisis, 212
Personal development plan, 231–232
Personal greed, 44
Personal leadership skills, development, 49–134
Personal time, 91–96
Personality tests, 99
Personnel issues, 140–147, 181–187
Planning, thinking and, 88–89
Planning process, leadership in well-rounded, 196
Position, authority, power, and leadership, 3–7, 14
Positive behavior, 130–131
Posner, Barry Z., 80
Potential, thinking and, 86–87
Power, leadership and, 2
Practice group system, 183
Practice succession, 223
Prejudice, addressing, 152
Presence, safety and trust, 129–133
Prior leaders, respect and learning from, 102, 108–111
Priorities, 74–75, 109, 113–114
Procedures, rules and, 156–160, 232–233
Procrastination, 74–79
Pushy voices, 77, 79

Q

Questions, open-ended, 81–82

R

Reagan, Ronald, 167
Reality, 53–58, 228
    Welch's six rules, 55–56
Recognition, public, 122–123, 146
Recruitment, changes in, 32
Requests, refusal of, 75
Resolution Works website, 164
Respect
    coaches and, 61
    non-authority members and, 148
    prior leaders, priority of, 109
    title and, 5–6
Responding to e-mail, 82–83
Response, negative, 142
Responsibility, 17–18, 190–191
Results, alignment principle and, 128

Retirement, planning for succession, 238–243
Retribution, resisting, 216
Riskin, Gerry, 78
Ritz-Carlton Corporation, shared authority, 120–121
Roles, noble possibilities in, 116–117
Roles, varying in law firms, 144–150
Roosevelt, Theodore, 67
Rubenstein, Herb, 8
Rudy, movie, 124–125
Rule 5.1, 190–193
Rules and professional conduct, 156–160

S

Sabbaticals, 93–94
Sande, Ken, 162
Sanders, J. Oswald, 108
Sandys, Celia, 129
Second innocence: Rediscovering Joy and Wonder, 116–117
Security, feeling of, 131–132, 214–215
Self education. *see* Education, leadership
Self-actualization, time off and, 93–94
Self-centered leadership, 12
Seminars and events, self education, 69
Servant leadership
    concept of, 8–13
    defined, 1–2
    discipline of, 132
    Morris Dees and, 66–67
    role of, 102
Service
    leadership and, 1–2
    to others, 12
    value, 8
Service to others
    authority figures and, 148
    without authority, 147
Services, development of, 230
Shared values, importance, and lack of, 119–120
Shelley, Marshall, 228
Sidley Austin law firm, 174–175
Silos, crisis of, 216–217
Sims, Peter, 91
Situations, difficult. *see* Crisis

Skills development, focus, 49
Smith, Senator Jefferson, role of, 138
Southern Poverty Law Center, 66–67
Special circumstances, Strategic planning and, 208
Spending, discretion, 120–121
Spiritual growth, 118
Staffing, changes in, 32–33
Stakeholder, mission and, 126–127
Stakeholders, pathfinding, 127
Standing up to others, courage to, 142
Stanley, Andy, 54–55, 59, 195
Stop doing list, 78
Straight from the Gut, 55–56
Strategic opportunities, 232–233
Strategic planning
    accomplishments, 201–202
    casting vision, 195–210
    commitment to, 206
    elements of, 198
    firm growth, types of, 228–235
    firm leader, role of, 198–202
    implementation, timing, 209–210
    involvement, appropriate, 203–210
    leadership of, 208
    obstacles to success-10, 208–10
    organizational system and, 205–207
    pitfalls, common, 199
    process of defining elements, 204
    shared values and, 119
    succession planning and, 222, 226
    teamwork and, 207
    work practices and, 206–207
Strategic thinking, 88–89
Strengths and weaknesses
    complementary, use of, 98
    crisis leadership and, 211–217
    diversity in in teamwork, 23
    personal, awareness of, 98–99
    principles of, 97–100
Structure, organizational
    changes in, 44
    typical, 10–13
Submission, principle of mutual, 131–132
Success
    danger of, 103
    defined, 101
    defined, Conrad Hilton, 101–102

definition, erroneous, 113
desire to see in others, 112–115
discipline 3, 101–115
guidelines, Conrad Hilton, 102
lies in the person, 49
organizational sharing and, 121–123
personal definition of, 93
Succession, defined, 222–223
Succession planning
actions for successful, 245–248
categories in process, 222–223
committee, permanent, 247–248
considerations, 239–241
crisis, avoiding, 223–224
death of member, 241
firm growth, components of, 230–235
groups, 247–248
individual plans and, 240–241
leadership roles and, 225–226
legacy of, 219–248
length of transition, 241
opportunities, evaluation of, 232–235
personnel involvement and, 225
successors, planning, 238–243
Successor, choosing, 244
Successors, developing capable, 238–243
Summit Law Group, 119
Support, importance of, 38
Susskind, Richard, 169
Synergy, teamwork and, 21
Systemic issues, 38

T

Taylor, William C., 165
Teams, reasons for using, 23–24
Teamwork
clients and, 172
concepts, 183–184
defined, 144–145
delegation and, 20
effective, principles of, 24–25
establishing opportunities, 22–23
ethics and, 190–193
firm members, 22–24
fostering environments, 183–184
no Grinch approach, 146

roles and contributions to, 145
service to others and, 112–115
strategic planning and, 207
trust and, 135
Technology, crisis and, 212–213
The Herbert Hoover Story, 27–28
The Lawyer's Guide to Professional Coaching, 60
The Servant Leader, 11
Thematic goal, defined, 211
Thinking, 86–89
Thinking for a Change, 86–87
Third party, succession planning and, 224–225
Thomas, R. Roosevelt, Jr., 151
Time, wasting, 94–95
Time, alone, 88–89
Time management, 74–79
Time off, 91–96
Timeliness, clients and, 170
Timing, failure and, 106
Training programs, 175–176
Transition
clients and, 241–242
length of, 241
succession planning, 223
successors, planning, 239
360° Leader Comprehensive Assessment, 99
Trust
admitting when wrong and, 142
attitudes and, 114
autonomy and, 134–164
conciliatory conflict resolution, 162–164
fostering, 16
gaining, 5–6
low trust environments, 136
sustained success and, 6
Trust, mutual, developing, 16–19
Trustworthiness, 25
Types of leadership, 1–2

U

Unbundling litigation, 42–43, 136
Underlying reasons, bad conduct, 141
Useful engagement, prior leaders and, 109

V

Values
    changes in, 30–31, 33–34
    core. see Core values
    crisis leadership and, 214
    firm, acceptance of, 119
    pathfinding and, 127
    priorities, changes in, 31
    shared. *see* Shared values
Violation, rules, 190–191
Virtual practices, 45
Vision
    casting, defined, 199–201
    crisis leadership and, 214
    defined, 195
    gauging decisions and, 108
    justifying the plan, 200
    principle of, 11–12
    reinforcing, 200–201
Voice, authentic, finding, 124–128

W

Wade, William J., 30
Weaknesses, evaluating, 99
Welch, Jack, 55–56, 244
Welch's six rules, 55–56
Wesemann, H. Edward, 203
Womble, Leadership program, 173–174
Womble Carlyle law firm, 173–174
Wood, Richard A. Jr., 8
Wooden, John, 101
Words, strength of, 16
Work practice, discontinuing, 206–207
Workaholic, defined, 91

X

Xenophon, 219

Y

Young lawyer training programs, 175–176

Z

Ziglar, Zig, 49

SELECTED BOOKS FROM

Google for Lawyers: Essential Search Tips and Productivity Tools
By Carole A. Levitt and Mark E. Rosch
Product Code: 5110704 • LPM Price: $47.95 • Regular Price: $79.95

This book introduces novice Internet searchers to the diverse collection of information locatable through Google. The book discusses the importance of including effective Google searching as part of a lawyer's due diligence, and cites case law that mandates that lawyers should use Google and other resources available on the Internet, where applicable. For intermediate and advanced users, the book unlocks the power of various advanced search strategies and hidden search features they might not be aware of.

LinkedIn in One Hour for Lawyers
By Dennis Kennedy and Allison C. Shields
Product Code: 5110737 • LPM Price: $19.95 • Regular Price: $34.95

Lawyers work in a world of networks, connections, referrals, and recommendations. For many lawyers, the success of these networks determines the success of their practice. LinkedIn®, the premier social networking tool for business, can help you create, nurture, and expand your professional network and gain clients in the process. LinkedIn® in One Hour for Lawyers provides an introduction to this powerful tool in terms that any attorney can understand. In just one hour, you will learn to:

- Set up a LinkedIn account
- Complete your basic profile
- Create a robust, dynamic profile that will attract clients
- Build your connections
- Use search tools to enhance your network
- Maximize your presence with features such as groups, updates, answers, and recommendations
- Monitor your network with ease
- Optimize your settings for privacy concerns
- Use LinkedIn® effectively in the hiring process
- Develop a LinkedIn strategy to grow your legal network

Facebook® in One Hour for Lawyers
By Dennis Kennedy and Allison C. Shields
Product Code: 5110745 • LPM Price: $24.95 • Regular Price: $39.95

With a few simple steps, lawyers can use Facebook® to market their services, grow their practices, and expand their legal network—all by using the same methods they already use to communicate with friends and family. *Facebook® in One Hour for Lawyers* will show any attorney—from Facebook® novices to advanced users—how to use this powerful tool for both professional and personal purposes.

The Electronic Evidence and Discovery Handbook: Forms, Checklists, and Guidelines
By Sharon D. Nelson, Bruce A. Olson, and John W. Simek
Product Code: 5110569 • LPM Price: $99.95 • Regular Price: $129.95

The use of electronic evidence has increased dramatically over the past few years, but many lawyers still struggle with the complexities of electronic discovery. This substantial book provides lawyers with the templates they need to frame their discovery requests and provides helpful advice on what they can subpoena. In addition to the ready-made forms, the authors also supply explanations to bring you up to speed on the electronic discovery field. The accompanying CD-ROM features over 70 forms, including, Motions for Protective Orders, Preservation and Spoliation Documents, Motions to Compel, Electronic Evidence Protocol Agreements, Requests for Production, Internet Services Agreements, and more. Also included is a full electronic evidence case digest with over 300 cases detailed!

Blogging in One Hour for Lawyers
By Ernie Svenson
Product Code: 5110744 • LPM Price: $24.95 • Regular Price: $39.95

Until a few years ago, only the largest firms could afford to engage an audience of millions. Now, lawyers in any size firm can reach a global audience at little to no cost—all because of blogs. An effective blog can help you promote your practice, become more "findable" online, and take charge of how you are perceived by clients, journalists and anyone who uses the Internet. Blogging in One Hour for Lawyers will show you how to create, maintain, and improve a legal blog—and gain new business opportunities along the way. In just one hour, you will learn to:

- Set up a blog quickly and easily
- Write blog posts that will attract clients
- Choose from various hosting options like Blogger, TypePad, and WordPress
- Make your blog friendly to search engines, increasing your ranking
- Tweak the design of your blog by adding customized banners and colors
- Easily send notice of your blog posts to Facebook and Twitter
- Monitor your blog's traffic with Google Analytics and other tools
- Avoid ethics problems that may result from having a legal blog

TO ORDER VISIT **WWW.SHOPABA.ORG** OR CALL 1-800-285-2221

Virtual Law Practice: How to Deliver Legal Services Online
By Stephanie L. Kimbro

Product Code: 5110707 • LPM Price: $47.95 • Regular Price: $79.95

The legal market has recently experienced a dramatic shift as lawyers seek out alternative methods of practicing law and providing more affordable legal services. Virtual law practice is revolutionizing the way the public receives legal services and how legal professionals work with clients. If you are interested in this form of practicing law, *Virtual Law Practice* will help you:

- Responsibly deliver legal services online to your clients
- Successfully set up and operate a virtual law office
- Establish a virtual law practice online through a secure, client-specific portal
- Manage and market your virtual law practice
- Understand state ethics and advisory opinions
- Find more flexibility and work/life balance in the legal profession

Social Media for Lawyers: The Next Frontier
By Carolyn Elefant and Nicole Black

Product Code: 5110710 • LPM Price: $47.95 • Regular Price: $79.95

The world of legal marketing has changed with the rise of social media sites such as Linkedin, Twitter, and Facebook. Law firms are seeking their companies attention with tweets, videos, blog posts, pictures, and online content. Social media is fast and delivers news at record pace. This book provides you with a practical, goal-centric approach to using social media in your law practice that will enable you to identify social media platforms and tools that fit your practice and implement them easily, efficiently, and ethically.

iPad Apps in One Hour for Lawyers
By Tom Mighell

Product Code: 5110739 • LPM Price: $19.95 • Regular Price: $34.95

At last count, there were more than 80,000 apps available for the iPad. Finding the best apps often can be an overwhelming, confusing, and frustrating process. iPad Apps in One Hour for Lawyers provides the "best of the best" apps that are essential for any law practice. In just one hour, you will learn about the apps most worthy of your time and attention. This book will describe how to buy, install, and update iPad apps, and help you:

- Find apps to get organized and improve your productivity
- Create, manage, and store documents on your iPad
- Choose the best apps for your law office, including litigation and billing apps
- Find the best news, reading, and reference apps
- Take your iPad on the road with apps for travelers
- Maximize your social networking power
- Have some fun with game and entertainment apps during your relaxation time

Twitter in One Hour for Lawyers
By Jared Correia

Product Code: 5110746 • LPM Price: $24.95 • Regular Price: $39.95

More lawyers than ever before are using Twitter to network with colleagues, attract clients, market their law firms, and even read the news. But to the uninitiated, Twitter's short messages, or tweets, can seem like they are written in a foreign language. Twitter in One Hour for Lawyers will demystify one of the most important social-media platforms of our time and teach you to tweet like an expert. In just one hour, you will learn to:

- Create a Twitter account and set up your profile
- Read tweets and understand Twitter jargon
- Write tweets—and send them at the appropriate time
- Gain an audience—follow and be followed
- Engage with other Twitters users
- Integrate Twitter into your firm's marketing plan
- Cross-post your tweets with other social media platforms like Facebook and LinkedIn
- Understand the relevant ethics, privacy, and security concerns
- Get the greatest possible return on your Twitter investment
- And much more!

The Lawyer's Essential Guide to Writing
By Marie Buckley

Product Code: 5110726 • LPM Price: $47.95 • Regular Price: $79.95

This is a readable, concrete guide to contemporary legal writing. Based on Marie Buckley's years of experience coaching lawyers, this book provides a systematic approach to all forms of written communication, from memoranda and briefs to e-mail and blogs. The book sets forth three principles for powerful writing and shows how to apply those principles to develop a clean and confident style.

iPad in One Hour for Lawyers, Second Edition
By Tom Mighell

Product Code: 5110747 • LPM Price: $24.95 • Regular Price: $39.95

Whether you are a new or a more advanced iPad user, *iPad in One Hour for Lawyers* takes a great deal of the mystery and confusion out of using your iPad. Ideal for lawyers who want to get up to speed swiftly, this book presents the essentials so you don't get bogged down in technical jargon and extraneous features and apps. In just six, short lessons, you'll learn how to:

- Quickly Navigate and Use the iPad User Interface
- Set Up Mail, Calendar, and Contacts
- Create and Use Folders to Multitask and Manage Apps
- Add Files to Your iPad, and Sync Them
- View and Manage Pleadings, Case Law, Contracts, and other Legal Documents
- Use Your iPad to Take Notes and Create Documents
- Use Legal-Specific Apps at Trial or in Doing Research

TO ORDER VISIT **WWW.SHOPABA.ORG** OR CALL 1-800-285-2221

30-DAY RISK-FREE ORDER FORM

Please print or type. To ship UPS, we must have your street address. If you list a P.O. Box, we will ship by U.S. Mail.

Name

Member ID

Firm/Organization

Street Address

City/State/Zip

Area Code/Phone (In case we have a question about your order)

E-mail

Method of Payment:
☐ Check enclosed, payable to American Bar Association
☐ MasterCard   ☐ Visa   ☐ American Express

Card Number   Expiration Date

Signature Required

MAIL THIS FORM TO:
American Bar Association, Publication Orders
P.O. Box 10892, Chicago, IL 60610

ORDER BY PHONE:
24 hours a day, 7 days a week:
Call 1-800-285-2221 to place a credit card order. We accept Visa, MasterCard, and American Express.

EMAIL ORDERS: orders@americanbar.org
FAX ORDERS: 1-312-988-5568

VISIT OUR WEB SITE: www.ShopABA.org
Allow 7-10 days for regular UPS delivery. Need it sooner? Ask about our overnight delivery options. Call the ABA Service Center at 1-800-285-2221 for more information.

GUARANTEE:
If—for any reason—you are not satisfied with your purchase, you may return it within 30 days of receipt for a refund of the price of the book(s). No questions asked.

Thank You For Your Order.

Join the ABA Law Practice Management Section today and receive a substantial discount on Section publications!

Product Code:	Description:	Quantity:	Price:	Total Price:
				$
				$
				$
				$
				$

Shipping/Handling:	
$0.00 to $9.99	add $0.00
$10.00 to $49.99	add $5.95
$50.00 to $99.99	add $7.95
$100.00 to $199.99	add $9.95
$200.00 to $499.99	add $12.95

*Tax:
IL residents add 9.25%
DC residents add 6%
Yes, I am an ABA member and would like to join the Law Practice Management Section today! (Add $50.00)

Subtotal:	$
*Tax:	$
**Shipping/Handling:	$
	$
Total:	$

TO ORDER VISIT **WWW.SHOPABA.ORG** OR CALL 1-800-285-2221

ABA Webstore: www.ShopABA.org

iTunes: www.apple.com/iTunes

LAW PRACTICE MANAGEMENT
RESOURCES FOR THE DIGITAL AGE

LPM e-books are now available to read on your iPad, smartphone, or favorite e-reader! To download the **latest releases** in EPUB or Apple format, visit the ABA Webstore or iTunes today. LPM's digital library is expanding quickly, so check back often for new e-book availability. Purchase LPM e-books today and be only **one click away** from the resources your law practice needs.

FOLLOW LPM!

Stay current with the latest news about LPM Books, including discount offers, free excerpts, author interviews, and more.

- t LPM Books Blog: http://lpmbooks.tumblr.com/
- t @LawPracticeTips
- f http://www.facebook.com/LawPracticeTips
- in ABA Law Practice Management Section Group